Planning
Small Town
America

Planning Small Town America

Observations, Sketches and a Reform Proposal

By
Kristina Ford
with
James Lopach
and
Dennis O'Donnell

For Richard

Contents

Acknowledgments

We wish to thank all the people who helped us conduct the research detailed in this book. First among these is Dr. Ray Murray, Associate Vice President for Research and Dean of the Graduate School at the University of Montana. Dr. Murray fostered the establishment of the Public Policy Research Institute at the University and wholeheartedly encouraged the research proposals which originated there. We are most grateful to him.

The Northwest Area Foundation supported the work with a generous grant to the Public Policy Research Institute. Many public officials and private individuals whose decisions affect land development were very kind in explaining their attitudes during lengthy interviews, and we again would like to express our appreciation for the time they gave this project. Other individuals offered singularly helpful guidance and information throughout the course of this research effort, including Joe Aldegarie, Mike Barton, Bruce Bender, Ray Conger, John DeVore, James Driscoll, Larry Johnson, Mike Kress, Marshall Kyle, Robb McCracken, Bruce Suenram, Chuck Stearns, Rachel Vielleux, and Susan Wallwork. We would particularly like to thank Janet Marko and Todd Johnson for their extraordinary and tireless help as research assistants.

Kristina Ford is indebted to early encouragement from Dick Netzer, Chester Rapkin, and George Sternlieb, three men whose distinguished professional lives inspire all of us who are planners to our best achievements.

Kristina Ford, James Lopach, and Dennis O'Donnell
Public Policy Research Institute
University of Montana, Missoula
September, 1989

Introduction

DANGEROUS LADY

A "Reader Comment" appeared one August morning in the Missoula, Montana, local newspaper. It read:

She's Capable But Dangerous

Kristina Ford, director of the Missoula Planning Office, has been on the job long enough to have her feet firmly planted in Missoula's bureaucracy. Those who know Kristina recognize that she is a smart, articulate, charming, pretty, and capable lady. She is very good at what she does (if you don't believe it, just watch her nice sidestep sometime). Besides all of this, she is a nice person. I truly like Kristina. Her generous qualities, however, obscure the fact that she may be the most dangerous thing to ever happen to the Missoula Valley.

The office over which Kristina presides, Planning, is not an agency which takes its job casually. The staff, under her capable direction, are very busy planning things and have no intentions of working in vain.

Too few people recognize that in order to implement all of these nicely drawn plans requires controlling people. Kristina's department would more appropriately be called the People Control Office. It has the size, muscle, autonomy, and budget to do just about whatever it wants, and what it wants is downright scary.

It could be that as a strong, capable, and aggressive manager of planning (control), Kristina represents a greater threat to the liberty and economic health of Missoula citizens than nuclear war, giardia, and spotted knapweed combined.

We are usually fortunate that we don't get as much government as we pay for, but this generality is obviously untrue in Kristina's case. She is a member of that group, which surfaces all too frequently in government, that believes there is no limit to man's (or woman's) capacity to govern others, and therefore, there should be no limitations which are begging to be imposed upon the citizens over whom government has authority (for their own good, of course).

It would be a blessing for all of us if some private employer would recognize the great worth of this capable lady, and steal her away to an honorable job in private business before she turns Missoula into the well-planned, well-regulated, well-controlled, and tyrannical utopia of which planners dream.—Gary S. Marbut, Missoula.[1]

No one reading Mr. Marbut's opinion over breakfast that morning could have been as startled as I, its subject, to learn of the extravagant threat I posed to Missoula—a rawboned western town set in an Ansel Adams environment. Outsiders who've heard its name probably know Missoula as home to the University of Montana, but this is no sedate college town. It is coarse-grained, a society of contractors and hot-tempered loggers, innkeepers and barmaids, realtors, professors, coeds and frat-boys, physicians, railroad men, conservationists, the Posse Comitatus, Rotarians and non-Rotarians, and the Freeholders—a group so certain of absolute property rights that it thinks only landowners should get a vote—and on and on.

But despite their antipathetic beliefs, these residents get along in relative peace and have even created a cohesive community. Society here is understood and conducted through a neo-western myth of recklessness and self-reliance, a myth which allows its subscribers to smooth over their contradictions, even to reconcile contrasts and conflicts. The conceit arises naturally. Montana is probably the most *western* of western states, home to ghost towns and site of Custer's last stand, backdrop to C. M. Russell's romantically heroic paintings. It is a state sparsely populated and remote, where working ranches surround towns, and where ordinary life goes on amid starkly imposing Rocky Mountain ranges. Even office workers lead vigorous lives, with their weekend backpacking in the wilderness areas, white water rafting on rivers traversed by Lewis and Clark, and pheasant hunting in grizzly bear habitats.

The myth celebrates and exaggerates more than the robust physical qualities of Missoulians. Townspeople are portrayed as self-reliant heroes living on the last frontier, a group of stern individualists vigilant against the unwelcome troubles of modern towns "back east," against governmental interference, and against the perceived loss of personal freedom to bureaucrats and needless laws. The myth is unifying.

Furthermore, it permits Missoulians to see the world as they would have it be, rather than as it is. Harmless, even amusing examples show up everywhere. Men dress like Gary Cooper in *High Noon* (he's from Montana, too), then drive to work at brokerage houses equipped with spaceage telecommunications devices. Families live on streets named Gunsight Court or Cowboy Gulch Road; teenagers attend Hellgate High. And for the last few years, bumper-stickers on pick-ups have blustered about gut-shooting newcomers at the border—this despite the mundane demographic fact that many people sporting it are newcomers themselves (nearly half the adult population in Montana moved here from elsewhere).

Some of these examples of the myth are trivial and harmless, and will undoubtedly fade as fashion changes and new slogans arrive. But Missoula's western myth works a pernicious effect when it precludes citizens from seeing that what they have built in Missoula is an American anyplace, and from realizing that if they continue to make reckless development decisions, they soon won't have a town worth mythologizing. Already, commercial franchises strike a garish line along the avenues, creating a pandemonium of familiar neon logos: Kentucky Fried Chicken, Best Western motels, Wendy's, McDonalds—you know them all and you'd find them anywhere. Prefab starter homes sit side by side, with no features to identify them with Montana save the license plates on cars parked out front. These houses, even these neighborhoods, could be in Indianapolis or Paterson, where many of the occupants grew up. The maple-shaded neighborhoods surrounding the university evidently took their design from the orderly street patterns of land-grant college towns in the midwest. The town's new sections, however, feature cul-de-sacs and oddly angled intersections that could only have been inspired by subdividers greedy for salable lots. Convenience stores, small-motor repair shops, and treeless parking lots form a patchwork among the grasslands that once made scenic the route out of town. All in all, a disinterested observer would not find the tracks of mankind in Missoula unique, nor even distinctive. Indeed, although the town fancies itself "The Brightest Star in the Big Sky," Missoula has been built like most other towns of its size.

Lewis Mumford's pretty phrase, that a city is where time becomes visible, provides an imaginative way of looking at man's constructions. By noticing the placement and design of individual buildings, we can see periods when towns were wealthy and when they were in decline; we can identify vernacular enthusiasms in architecture. We can deduce how family life was conducted in different eras—the number of people in a household, where their children went to school, and who lived nearby. We can even see how municipal decisions have been made. In Missoula, development in the last 35 years has strewn ranch-style houses, trailer parks, log cabin bars, convenience shops, and second-hand stores in a loose disarray. The city and its suburban areas have taken on the predictable form that results from a simple municipal logic which says that growth—any growth, anywhere, under any circumstance—means economic progress and should be approved. Traffic jams, excessive and expensive road maintenance costs, a scarred environment, and houses in the pathway of floods are all part of Missoula, just as they are wherever permissive attitudes toward growth exist.

The many misfortunes of Missoula, the very problems I had been schooled to forestall with techniques that I later taught graduate students, are standard post-World War II problems of population growth. Look at Missoula without the template of its romantic myth, and you would undoubtedly agree that the single unique quality here is a sternly majestic landscape that puts in high profile the mindless improvidence of a familiar American jumble. In a commonplace modern paradox, the very landscape that makes Missoula a uniquely compelling place to live is threatened by poor development decisions made to accommodate people wanting to live there.

I came to Missoula to be the director of the Planning Department, which has a say in virtually everything having to do with how people use land in Missoula and Missoula County. That meant 76,000 people in a 2,100 square mile area, 2 percent of which is purely urban and 98 percent of which is Western rural: 5-acre ranchettes, gravel pits, wilderness areas, national forests, trailer parks, timber lots, and 30,000-acre cattle ranches still owned and overseen by tough, white-haired old men on palaminos. Running the department capably meant telling a cowboy entrepreneur he couldn't build his stockcar track next to the stucco duplexes he already owned and rented out cheap; or telling a gypo he must not connect natural gas to his double-wide with PVC pipe. Or standing up to headstrong land developers with big Las Vegas backing and telling them they couldn't subdivide their hillside unless they allowed fire trucks a route to get up the grade. These, in fact, were the easy arguments. The hard ones were about policies with less obvious payoffs: discouraging sprawl, keeping lakes open to public access, getting sidewalks built, conserving hillsides before they got developed.

What I found during two years in Missoula was that to most ordinary citizens and many of their elected leaders, planning is a discipline unlike most professions. It really has to argue its existence every time it asks to be taken seriously, and it has to do a good deal more than argue well. It must continually regenerate itself, and do so against a tradition of antagonism. This state has never encouraged planning—planning costs money, and Montana rarely has very much for very long. And for that reason, history here is a sad repetition of laissez-faire exploitation of the land's riches. Opponents of planning, public officials and citizens alike, think planners are dangerous—or worse, that they are dreamers.

Mr. Marbut's letter was cheered by antiplanning factions in Missoula, laughed at by planning partisans, ignored by most readers, and forgotten by the time the next morning's edition appeared. I did not forget it, and not simply because it was about me—although that unquestionably kept it in my mind. It was the letter's opinion about planning, and the reception that view received in the community, which I found memorable. Together, they dramatize several noteworthy facts of planning in Missoula, and in other American municipalities as well.

Disregard the letter's errors of exaggeration and misrepresentation, disregard particulars topical in Montana at the time it was written (giardia and knapweed), even disregard its failure to specify *what*, exactly, I had done that was so frightening. What remains is a clear message of hostility that accurately describes the attitude of many people with vested interests in land development. Bankers, realtors, landowners, and builders—people whose livelihood depends on development—number among them. The individuals in this group may be few, but they enlist sympathizers by dressing up their financial interests in growth as first principles of freedom. This strategy plays to the sentiments of people without investments at stake who are willing to listen. The American public is generally apprehensive about taking advice from unelected experts, about losing individual autonomy to government, even about elected leaders' judgments of what best serves the public interest. And when planning gets represented as the embodiment of these fears—no matter the motives of those doing the representing—a politically powerful antiplanning constituency results.

The fact that Mr. Marbut's opinion was dismissed as risible by many of its readers in Missoula suggests a companion point about contemporary planning. Planners work on behalf of a public mostly unconcerned and largely unfamiliar with the day-to-day routine of land use decisions. Busy earning livelihoods from enterprises not connected with the land, most people want local government invisible and reliable, and they ask only that it provide an untroubled atmosphere in which private life can flourish. They have little time for writing letters to the editor, for learning how land use decisions get made, or for appearing at contentious public hearings. Their support for planning, to the extent it exists at all, reduces to a sentiment that good planning is necessary work and somebody ought to do it.

In practical terms, this means that on the occasions when citizens appear at public hearings to criticize particular development proposals, they have little more than an impressionistic knowledge of land management practices and planning principles. Their arguments prove no match for the firsthand knowledge of developers whose business is to anticipate and counter criticism of their proposals. Planning support usually appears as emotional and short-lived enthusiasms of laymen—for a new park or a well-designed roadway, or for solutions to newly discovered problems. The development community's opposition to planning, on the other hand, is methodical and expert in its appeals to local leaders. Opposition often takes the form of well-rehearsed arguments which, rather than addressing the concerns that planners have raised, commend particular development proposals as essential to a local government's ability to encourage economic opportunity, increase employment, or sweeten property tax receipts. The advice of planners then seems to stand alone, to be trivial as compared to government's larger concerns, or to represent a position backed only by uninformed partisans. Elected officials find such advice easy to ignore.

On a related matter, the opinion printed in the newspaper reveals a common misunderstanding of the intentions of sound land use management. Mr. Marbut takes the ultimate goal of planning to be a sort of rationalism gone mad: "The well-planned, well-regulated, well-controlled and tyrannical utopia of which planners dream." For many people, of course, the word *planning* implies grand schemes: building Pruitt-Igoe, designing BART, tearing Pruitt-Igoe down. To most, planning is mysterious, overcomplicated, and superfluous—hard to "see." In fact, of course, a planner's notion for a better society is graspable in the small terms of requiring a land developer to install sidewalks and culverts, or preserving land for parks. It is the compilation of little decisions that makes a town well planned and citizens' lives rewarding.

But this prosaic fact, while a crucial underpinning to the practice of planning, has not been explained publicly in most towns. If planners are to get effective allies, they must explain what planning is in simple terms, rather than by describing overwhelming or unrealistic visions of the future.

Antagonism toward planning, misunderstanding of its aims, and the absence of effective support—all together—help explain the fact that bad land use decisions get made anew year after year, in town after town. Wherever this occurs, planners' advice has been effectively discounted. Perhaps Mr. Marbut perceived that these traditional barriers to planning were being broken, and that a constituency able to make planning an estimable force was forming in Missoula. Judging from the tone of his letter, Mr. Marbut apparently believed this change resulted from some personal characteristics that enabled the planning director to enlist effective allies. His opinion is not unique, even among planners. In fact, what might be termed the personality theory of effectiveness has been argued in several books about making city planning "work." But it is not a particularly useful or constructive conceit, since it provides little specific advice for making a planning staff effective. More useful would be identifying something basic to the practice of planning that could be changed. In this way, good land use decisions arguably could result— not because a well-trained planner happened to have a compelling personality, but because the advice any well-trained planner could give decisionmakers was itself compelling. If such a possibility exists, it could make systematic what has often seemed merely accidental.

The letter naturally occasioned my self-appraisal of two years as planning director, an experience which I could most responsibly credit as a moderate success. It had been an engaging professional assignment with large battles, small triumphs, small defeats . . . and continual frustration at local leaders who were either unwilling or unable to make consistently good decisions. But I had little interest in re-enacting the commonplace battles waged in Montana, or in brooding about personal comments made about me in the newspaper. Rather, I wanted to speculate about the causes of planning's weakness and to consider ways to make planning and growth management work better. I had several ideas for improvement, and even the beginnings of an idea for a method which could, I thought, join the interests of developers, planners, citizens, and governmental officials. To help sharpen my various ideas and notions, I enlisted the efforts of James Lopach, a political scientist, and Dennis O'Donnell, an economist. Professor Lopach has considerable experience working with state and local governments on questions of institutional structure and legal authorization; Professor O'Donnell has extensive experience dealing with development issues and with analyzing incremental costs of public utilities. Together, they brought to the project the disciplinary rigors of their respective fields, an enthusiasm for the project, knowledge of other places, and diligent application of effort on behalf of making planning more effective in Missoula, in Montana, and in small towns everywhere.

We believe, and will argue in the following chapters, that the antagonism toward planning expressed by Mr. Marbut, the skepticism that greets planners' advice, the ambivalence many citizens feel toward planning, and the continuance of bad development decisions are all situations that can be improved. This book offers our suggestions. Chapter 1 describes how enabling legislation for planning envisions the way land use decisions should be made as towns grow and change; Chapter 2 describes how these decisions actually do get made, suggesting weaknesses in the ideal conception. Both of these chapters rely on my experience as a teacher, researcher, and planning director.

Throughout these early chapters appear quotations from contemporary writers as well as short sketches of planning practice at the local government level. These are meant to show the reader concrete examples of some points made in the essay, and to suggest how American towns are perceived by observers untrained in the planning profession. By including these quotations and sketches, we intend to enrich planners' powers of observation, a talent exemplified by one of America's foremost essayists, Henry James. An important side of his genius has been said to be his susceptibility to "the look of things, the look that conveys their meaning, to catch the colour, the relief, the expression, the surface, the substance of the human spectacle."[2] A similar susceptibility to surroundings is crucial to planners, as the concluding chapter will argue. These quotations and sketches are meant to enliven your reading of the arguments presented in the early chapters and are placed where there is a clear link with the text. They can also be read separately, as musings in expressive language about the world that thoughtful laymen see—and practicing planners confront.

Chapters 3, 4, and 5 describe the work done by all three of us and will introduce a new means of evaluating development projects that have been proposed in small towns. We believe this tool will result in planners' advice being more effective. The final chapter summarizes the work and suggests an attitude toward the hard task of being a local governmental planner that might make the job more productive.

NOTES

1. "Missoulian," August 22, 1984, p.5.
2. Alfred Kazin, *A Writer's America:* *Landscape in Literature* (New York: Alfred A. Knopf, 1988), p. 128.

1

Contemporary Townscapes: A Confluence of Land Use Decisions

American towns commemorate decisions made about how to use land: they have been shaped by commercial enthusiasms, contractors' calculations of profit, and by domestic aspiration and accomplishment. Consider your town. You may not be aware that many pleasing attributes of where you live issued from land use decisions. Perhaps trucks from the local sawmill can enter an expressway without going through town, or people who live in a retirement home can walk out their front door to catch a city bus, or children can get to a playground without being driven. Most people take for granted these ordinary satisfactions of community life, but in fact each example resulted from individual parcels of land being developed with a thought about how their ultimate use would interact with other developed lands. The playground was not located where there are no houses; the retirement home was sited with a thought to how its residents might get around in the city, and so forth.

You are probably more aware of the disappointing features of land use decisions. On the outskirts of your town, you're likely to see treeless housing tracts haphazardly situated amidst working farms; downtown, shops might be boarded up while new regional shopping centers thrive; going to and from work, you probably endure lengthy traffic tieups at unavoidable junctions. You might also realize that these familiar vexations arose in obvious ways from approvals given to develop parcels of land. Your elected leaders had to give their sanction before farmland could be subdivided and shopping centers could be built. They even had to approve the construction of each shop along a commercial strip where streets were already congested.

Even if development in your town has brought none of these modern annoyances, natural features of where you live have probably been tainted. New subdivisions might have opened, inadvertantly contaminating or depleting aquifers in the region. Small streams may have filled with silt as bulldozers readied land for construction; air pollution may have increased as commuters drive longer distances to housing developments. And if none of these apply, an afternoon spent reading your local newspaper will undoubtedly disclose more particularized examples of environmental ugliness—wells polluted, rare vegetation destroyed, or natural nesting areas for migratory birds depleted.

Land use decisions can also create negative economic effects, often in the form of unnecessarily high local taxes. For example, a special levy might be imposed because a new subdivision requires the construction of an additional fire station despite excess firefighting capacity downtown. Local taxes might include levies to pay for water lines extended to serve a private developer's proposed industrial park. The pipes may not even be used—though they must be paid for—if the developer's plans evaporate with an unfortunate turn in the business cycle. Line-item scrutiny of a local government's budget will show these economic effects of land use decisions. Tax increases at the very least annoy most citizens, but they can have more serious consequences as well. They undermine the public's confidence in elected leaders' ability to manage the budget, they can cause towns to shoulder unnecessarily burdensome public debts, and they can even impoverish a person of limited means.

Land use decisions can also discriminate unfairly against poorer residents. Local leaders can exercise considerable discretion over what sort of housing can be built in a town, where it can be sited, and the specific construction conditions that must be fulfilled. In many towns, leaders have used such powers to separate relatively inexpensive types of housing from more costly homes. For example, mobile home parks are likely to be found in districts not only without real parks, but without trees, lawns, or shrubbery. Typically, they are sited on vacant land adjacent to highways, where residents will suffer noise, dust, and motor vehicle exhaust; they are even in low-lying areas that flood periodically. All such places are a jumble with hazards to domestic life, particularly to children who may have neither suitable places to play nor safe walkways to school. A prominent attorney satirized the attitude of towns where economic segregation has resulted from land use decisions:

> Low-income people have a constitutional right to live at high densities on the most worthless land having the worst possible environmental conditions as long as the land is "properly buffered" from any place they might possibly want to go.[1]

That is, poorer citizens in these towns are kept apart, reminded by their surroundings of their civic powerlessness.

However, the point of this discussion is not to catalog complaints, but to reveal their shared attribute: each example resulted from a municipal approval given to a private person to develop a tract of land. Perhaps most disappointing is the simple fact that better development decisions could have avoided most of the offensive results. Townscapes are compilations of land use decisions, and many good decisions have indeed been made in American towns. Wherever traffic moves easily through commercial districts, where children have safe places to walk and play, where a variety of development and some balance between nature and building are present, and where local tax levies do not have to support unnecessary extension of public services—there land use choices were made well. Effecting more of these decisions is the subject of this book.

Observations About What Americans Have Built

. . . All over the county, townhouses and condominiums were devouring orchards and vineyards just as they'd devoured the potato farms on Long Island, and whenever I saw a sign for a new subdivision, Eternal Now Villas, Cypress Estates where no cypresses had ever grown, or read about the Corps of Engineers' plan to dam the river, or saw bulldozers or sewer pipes or even surveyors, I flew into a rage. The assault was relentless, without purpose, another aspect of disease.[2]

Bill Barich

Missoula, Montana, portrays many ordinary land use decisions, good and bad, that can be found in small, relatively slow growing towns in the country. Missoula spreads from the Hellgate Canyon into a broad valley at the junction of the Blackfoot, Clark Fork, and Bitterroot rivers. The city has acquired land along the Clark Fork River's course through town and has landscaped and lighted a walkway along its banks. Old train stations downtown have found productive commercial uses, and two old hotels have been adroitly rehabilitated to house low-income tenants. Mountains surround the town so closely, in fact, that the entrance to the Rattlesnake National Wilderness Area is one mile from a stop on the city bus line. This beauty owns a practical side, for tourism is a major support of Missoula's economy. People come here to enjoy the recreational life the surroundings provide, and they stay here for the same reason.

Missoula is a town that has made irreversible decisions. Typical of much of the West, the lower hillsides and flat ranchlands have been haphazardly developed into residential tracts or 5-acre "ranchettes." Roads to hillside houses scar the land, and in this semi-arid country years will pass before vegetation can soften the raw look of newly laid streets. Strip commercial establishments sprawl among weedlots beside the highways, so that to see the mountains you have to peer between loud billboards and the neon trademarks of national fast-food franchises. But that's only when you *can* see the mountains: in the winter they often disappear into a brown haze of air pollution. In short, the people seem bent on ruining the very qualities that attracted them in the first place.

As I've said already, this description sounds a lot like countless towns and cities across the country. The inquiry that resulted in this book could have started in any of these communities: why do the same decisions get made so often and in so many places when their results are so predictably bad? To answer this question, it is useful first to distinguish between two different areas in contemporary towns.

WHERE LAND USE DECISIONS ARE MADE

Bad land use decisions appear in highest relief in the urban fringe—the area you pass through when you drive into almost any town. Scattered across the landscape in no discernible order might be a subdivision, a fallow field, a gas station, an expanse of weeds where "For Sale" signs blister in the sun, a convenience store, a working farm, even a small industrial plant. The fringe area has been and probably will always be the principal locus of growth in America. In part, this is the result of simple economics: the land available here comes in large parcels and at prices below those asked for more central locations. Prices in town are higher because public utilities already extend to urban tracts and access to roadways is established. Furthermore, the profitability of a centrally located venture seems more assured: market patterns can be more or less accurately gauged, and demand for some particular product or service can be estimated. Buying land in the urban fringe is riskier and preparing it for development is more expensive than buying acreage downtown, and the price of land reflects these facts.

Developers prefer the fringe because experience has taught them that projects proposed there will be approved more readily than proposals made on land in the well-settled sections of local jurisdictions, where the discretion officials exercise is limited by several factors: buildings exist, streets have been laid, relationships among the uses are ingrained, and there is even some consensus among individuals as to how they would see their neighborhood change. In such places there exists a shared sense—however inchoate—of a "character." The more completely citizens in a neighborhood can agree on that character and on the uses detrimental to it—apartment buildings or mobile homes—the more likely they can argue their point of view articulately and effectively. Accompanying these citizens' appearance at public hearings is a united political will that no elected leader can ignore. In essence, neighbors ask leaders to protect their neighborhood, and, as a matter of practical politics, leaders do.

Developers have learned to avoid proposing projects where residents seem to have agreed about what threatens the nature of their neighborhood. As a result, most choices regarding land in established and cohesive neighborhoods are simply adjustments to existing uses, made to accommodate new demographic trends or to prevent nuisances from recurring. If a town's population ages, its leaders might be asked to amend zoning regulations so as to allow "mother-in-law" apartments in a district formerly restricted to single-family houses. If citizens complain that they can not find parking spaces near their homes because of increased commercial traffic in the neighborhood, the town might start requiring offstreet parking for stores in residential areas. These are small decisions, likely to be acceptable within individual neighborhoods.

Sketches of Planning Practice

Shrinking from Neighborhood Opposition

The perennial problem of finding a location for low-income housing that will not generate neighborhood opposition has recurred with particular virulence over shelters for homeless persons, and prompted some tactless solutions. For example, the Human Resources Administration in New York City proposed using ships as floating shelters to avoid neighborhood opposition to permanent locations; Mayor Larry Agran of Irvine, California, offered quarters in a renovated dog pound.[3]

The Urban Protectorate

Neighborhoods where citizens agree on qualities worth preserving might well be called the *urban protectorate.* In these areas, residents expect government either to maintain the status quo, or to allow only changes that enhance whatever quality of the district they particularly value. By being unwilling to force an unpopular use on a united neighborhood, elected leaders protect the wishes of that section of town. Ultimately, the effect of this protection is that developers look for sites elsewhere, and vacant land in the protectorate goes undeveloped.

However, as any student of municipal finance or urban planning knows, many of the vacant lots in already urbanized areas should be developed. Rationally speaking, more compact development—without sacrifice of adequate open space—would reduce energy costs by requiring fewer auto trips, reduce the necessity of extending public services, reduce the pressure to develop environmentally sensitive or agricultural land, and make it easier to provide public transportation. When development reaches out into new territory, these opportunities to offer services more efficiently and to protect valuable undeveloped land are lost.

There is also an insidious side to the urban protectorate. While its residents may be well organized and articulate, able to defend their neighborhood against what they see as an incursion of undesirable uses, residents elsewhere either may not be as articulate or may not be aware of their latent political power. For any of a variety of reasons—apathy, poverty, and lack of political astuteness—people in these neighborhoods do not protect themselves from changes they might find undesirable. Such neighborhoods become, in effect, dumping grounds for the noxious uses that more politically potent areas can prevent. As a few hours perusing planning journals would tell, offending uses are pretty much the same across the country. They include any residential structure other than a detached house, commercial establishments in settled neighborhoods, mobile homes, and group homes. And the arguments against them are essentially invariant—they will attract undesirable people, disrupt an area's harmony, or harm nearby property values. Planners are not insensitive to these concerns: rather, they try to argue that undesirable uses should be spread about town rather than grouped to create zones of urban ugliness.

Discerning what, exactly, residents of even the most cohesive neighborhood want defended can be difficult. Different residents can have surprisingly various ideas about their neighborhood's essential character, and very dissimilar notions about how a vacant tract should be developed. Parents might prefer no development at all, so that their children can continue playing in the open lot. Those willing to see the land developed typically have in mind only the uses they personally desire. Parents with young children may prefer a daycare center; young professionals may prefer a Chinese takeout restaurant; older people may want a community center—and each person or group may vehemently dislike and intend to forestall what the others prefer. Rather than first trying to ascertain all the private desires in a neighborhood and then imagining a project that could respond, developers look for land elsewhere.

The value of planning is easily demonstrated by pointing out examples of where it has been ignored. Unfortunately for this type of argument, bad land use decisions in the urban protectorate take on a lower profile than in the urban fringe. If you see a cluster of duplexes marooned among trucking docks, or children with nowhere to play but broken-down warehouses, chances are you are seeing refugees of decisions made to keep less expensive houses out of the urban protectorate. Or if you see a group home for the elderly being built on the outskirts of a town that affords ample vacant land nearer the city center, you might be seeing the results of elected leaders protecting a neighborhood's sense of itself as a district of single-family houses. However, in these examples the connection between protective decisions in one place and development in another is not immediately discernible.

In fact, some consequences of land use decisions in the urban protectorate are virtually invisible. On the outskirts of town you might notice an apartment building going up where there are no public services. What you might not notice is the vacant tract in the middle of town where the apartments were originally proposed. And even if you did notice the vacant parcel, you could not see the sewer and water lines, the electricity lines, and the natural gas pipes buried along its perimeter —all underused and installed at public expense. Neither might you notice that the land lies on a city bus route. The fact that the apartment building is not going up on this land might be the result of a land use decision made in the protectorate, but that conclusion cannot be reached simply by looking at development patterns. What this discussion means is that countering the opposition of established neighborhoods to development can not often be based on a readily demonstrable logic.

For reasons of rationality in the delivery of public services, for reasons of reducing pressure to develop scenic or agricultural land, as well as for reasons of spreading less desirable uses proportionately about town, planners should be able to use their professional expertise to argue for new construction in the urban protectorate. That they cannot, or have not, is evident from reading the proceedings of public hearings in which otherwise suitable building proposals were denied in the most obviously developable parts of town.

The Urban Frontier

Developers prefer to imagine projects on the fringe of existing urbanization, an area that might aptly be called the *urban frontier*. Settled sporadically, this area rarely constitutes a cohesive neighborhood. Rather than speaking about common wishes, private landowners argue their property rights with hyperbolized rhetoric and remain skeptical about governmental guidance of growth. There is little common sentiment about how the remaining vacant land might best be used, and in fact, disagreements over land often become vicious battles. Consequently, on the territories surrounding American towns lie most of the sad results worked by greed, lack of foresight, and uncoordinated decisions regarding the use of land. All are qualities reminiscent of the American frontier in the nineteenth century.

However, unlike that disappeared and now idealized frontier, the urban frontier will continue to exist, and its disappointing elements are not the stuff of idealization. The contemporary frontier can be found in the partially developed environs of each and every American town, no matter how small the town nor how apparently tranquil the land. When growth comes to these towns, the existing frontiers will gradually fill up

with new development and become more fully urbanized. As this
happens, some growth will spread to the land beyond—the land as yet
undeveloped—and that area will become the new frontier.

The range of options for how to use land that lies beyond towns is
virtually unlimited. Consequently, elected officials see a wide variety of
proposals, but have little of the guidance customarily afforded by
preexisting developments and long-standing relationships among users
of land. Furthermore, the interests people have in how individual tracts
might be used are largely unknown, and often quite disharmonious.
Take, as an example, a flat, well-drained pasture on prime agricultural
soil. Its owner may see the plain as a capital investment that will be sold
someday to afford a handsome retirement. An entrepreneur may envision a man-made lake lined with expensive homes. Commuters who
pass by, however, might prefer that the pasture remain undeveloped
because deer graze there or wildflowers bloom—or simply because it
affords a visual respite from man-made features. Environmentalists
might argue for keeping the pasture in its natural state, not for its
beauty but because it recharges the local aquifer. We know that choosing
what to do with this tract, should the owner decide to sell, will impli-
cate all affected interests. Moreover, choosing what to do with the
land also will affect the interests of townspeople who've never noticed
the pasture: their property taxes, to name the most obvious concern,
might increase if public services must be extended once development
occurs.

All that is known, then, about making good land use decisions should
come to bear at the urban frontier before development occurs, and
should inform both private parties and public authorities. For at that
early point, the results of alternative development schemes can be
projected, and choices can be made that respond to the widest assortment of public and private concerns. And even if local officials were not
to rely on such an analytical approach, they should be open to guiding
growth on the urban frontier so as to avoid repeating mistakes made
elsewhere so often.

Informed citizens and their elected leaders have known for a long time
the harmful results of land use decisions badly made. It seems reasonable to expect that local leaders would be able to prevent environmental
degradation, provide agreeable circumstances for all social classes, and
foresee the economic consequences of development. However, as predictable and obviously harmful as the results of bad land use decisions
may seem, they get made over and over again because they originate in

American traditions of governance which give sanctity to local discretion and control.

Observations About What Americans Have Built

About half way between West Egg and New York the motor road hastily joins the railroad and runs beside it for a quarter of a mile, so as to shrink away from a certain desolate area of land. This is a valley of ashes—a fantastic farm where ashes grow like wheat into ridges and hills and grotesque gardens; where ashes take the forms of houses and chimneys and rising smoke and, finally, with a transcendent effort, of men who move dimly and already crumbling through the powdery air.[4]

F. Scott Fitzgerald

HOW THINGS ARE SUPPOSED TO WORK

To understand how bad decisions are made, you need first understand how decisions are supposed to be made. The remainder of this chapter will offer some preliminary information on this subject. First will be a discussion of the decisionmaking structure for land use decisions; second, there will be a description of the professional tools that planners use when they try to advise elected leaders about managing the use of land; and lastly there will be an explanation of the logic that guides municipalities' ultimate decisions about how land can be used. The following sections are synopses of very complicated matters. The interested reader can consult standard planning texts for a fuller discussion of the important concepts that this chapter will briefly raise.

Decisionmaking Structure for Land Use Decisions

States, which designate the duties of towns, cities, counties, and villages, customarily give authority over land use matters to these local governments because development of land seems a very parochial matter. Local governments, the state believes, know more about development issues and can be most responsive to them. The provisos under which local jurisdictions plan for and then permit the use of land exist in state-enabling legislation, the legal means by which states confer powers to local governments.

Enabling acts throughout the country read virtually as they did in

1928, the year the U.S. Department of Commerce published the Standard City Planning Enabling Act for states to use in setting up the mechanism by which growth and land use change could be managed. The law put forward principles of local planning, based on progressive reform efforts to correct obvious deficiencies in local government. Enlightened by revelations of corruption in big city machine politics, and inspired by the vision of urban beauty and order they had seen at the White City at the world's Columbian Exposition, reformers in this era placed their faith in new technical solutions to society's problems. Skilled civic-minded professionals, they believed, could design beautiful cities that would supplant the slums that had come with industrialization in the nation's urban centers. The reformers also believed that planners had to be removed from the corrupting influence of politicians.[5]

In the first 25 years of the twentieth century, good government enthusiasts experimented with various tools, laws, and principles to bring the fledgling profession of planning to maturity. Their work was the subject of journal articles, professional meetings, and innumerable court cases, all of which eventuated in the Standard Act of 1928. Subsequently, the proposals for reform contained in the act were voted up by electorates across the nation. Cities hired planners who had trained as landscape architects and engineers, and following the standard enabling act's stipulations, put them to work for independent planning commissions rather than for elected officials.

An important function of these commissions, also known as planning boards, was to protect the planning function from political pressure. Even the most convinced proponents of planning didn't believe the planning staff would be popular. Planners work from a comprehensive plan which, by designating appropriate uses of undeveloped land, expresses a community's desires for its future development. This means that plans characteristically restrict specific activities to locations the town as a whole considers suitable. Naturally, individuals who own property at these locations have ideas for how they can use their land for pleasure or profit or both, and their ideas frequently conflict with those of the community. As a consequence, proponents of planning could foresee that constituents would on occasion pressure local politicians to change the plan or to interpret the plan's stipulations in favor of a single individual, or even get rid of the planners altogether. These proponents also knew that politicians would in all likelihood not protect the planning staff. Planners' advice, after all, always assumes the longer view, while political leaders typically seize issues delimited by election dates, such as increasing the tax base and providing jobs for voters. Indeed, in controversies over appropriate development, many politicians find planners to be a further complication to an already difficult problem. For all these reasons, the notion of an independent planning commission was advocated as the ideal organization for local government planning because it could shield planners from political vulnerability.[6]

The second important purpose of independent commissions was to inspire support for the activity of planning among members of the general community, particularly among owners of property. Then, as now, planners' expertise was understood as likely to restrict individual exercise of property rights. Proponents of planning believed that a reduction in individual rights could serve not only the public interest, but, in fact, could improve the value of each individual's land by making a town more attractive as a place to do business and to live. Consequently, commissioners were chosen because they were prominent businessmen who could convince their peers that a well-planned community would enjoy increased property values.

As planning gradually became accepted as a part of local government and as land use controls survived early judicial scrutiny, independent planning commissions found another reason for existence. With the increased powers enjoyed by planners, commissions have become bodies that temper the professional planning staff's views about appropriate development and land use. Chosen to represent the various interests existing in any given town, commissioners moderate the staff's advice for how the community should change, what is a sound land use decision, what is fair, and what is politically practicable. A developer might propose a convenience shop in a residential neighborhood. Because his design complies with all pertinent zoning requirements, the planning staff recommends approval. However, when the commission holds a public hearing on the matter, neighbors say that headlights from cars coming to the shop late at night will disturb their sleep. Sympathetic to this testimony, the planning commission might impose conditions to its approval of the project. The developer might be asked to limit the store's hours of operation, or to provide additional landscaping to buffer the shop from neighboring houses, or even to design a different entrance for cars. This example portrays the best realization of an independent commission: it represents the whole community, and it keeps the comprehensive plan and planners' advice in harmony with legitimate individual concerns.[7]

Planning commissions enjoy an independent position in local government, whether or not they actually serve the purposes described above. State law defines their formal duties as advising the local elected leaders who choose them, and overseeing the planning department. To perform the latter function, the commission characteristically hires a planning director, who supervises the staff as it performs such daily planning activities as issuing building permits, explaining zoning ordinances, listening to complaints about land uses and controls, or interpreting the comprehensive plan. On planning matters which require votes by local governing bodies—zoning changes, subdivision approvals, adoption of comprehensive plans—the commission hears staff reports and public testimony on the matter at hand, then makes nonbinding recommendations for action to elected officials. For their part, these officials read the staff reports and the testimony from the hearing conducted by the planning commission, consider the commission's recommendations, and then hold their own public hearing before reaching a final conclusion. This process is called the two-hearing process for reaching land use decisions and it is typical of how such decisions are made throughout the country.

This, briefly, is the administrative structure within which planning advice is given to elected officials who ultimately must decide land use matters. Once the elected officials have made a decision to adopt a plan, to enact land use controls, or to allow a proposed development to be built, they delegate to the planning staff the authority for seeing a final decision carried out. The next portion of the chapter will describe the tools planners rely on for making their recommendations on land use matters, and the final section will discuss the municipal logic that affects how such matters are decided.

Planning Tools: Guiding the Use of Land

From their respective states, local jurisdictions have been given authority to plan the use of land and to ensure plans will be followed. These powers follow logically from the three-step paradigm that most states believe local jurisdictions follow when making land use decisions. First, a town adopts a plan showing how land *should* be used; second, local leaders carry out this plan by legislating how land *can* be used; and third, as development occurs, land *is* used according to the plan's designations.

Under this paradigmatic process, the town-as-planned becomes the town-as-built. Each step will be described below.

Paradigmatic Step 1: The Comprehensive Plan.   A community's comprehensive plan—also called its master plan—is the foundation for guiding how land should be used. The plan joins facts and opinions about a community with projections and aspirations for its future. The pertinent facts describe inhabitants of a town and their environment, and form an inventory of current conditions. Included are demographic and economic specifics of townspeople—their numbers in different age groups, the types of households they live in, where they work, and how much money they make—all facts determinant of the basic human needs a town seeks to satisfy. In addition, facts are compiled regarding where people live and under what conditions, where their children go to school, where families spend their leisure time, and the transportation individuals use to get around to their daily activities. This inventory of current conditions depicts how life is lived in a town.

Opinions about that life naturally form the basis of a town's plan for its future, and to this end, citizens and public officials are invited to speak their mind about civic life. In a collected form, these opinions catalogue the satisfactions a town provides its citizens, as well as the environmental, social, or economic disappointments people suffer because of the way land has been used in their community. Once carefully gathered and analyzed, these facts and opinions offer a reliable sense of how things are, locally, and what issues are of the greatest importance there.

To this depiction of how things are, the plan attaches relevant projections about what the future might bring and how land uses will be affected. The plan forecasts changes a town might expect in its economic activity: what industries are likely to come to town, or leave; how existing commerce will improve or worsen; and how employment opportunities will be affected. Such economic activities themselves make demands on land, and they also cause changes in a town's population that might affect land.

A simple example will show the connection. If new industries come to town, they might need new buildings, and perhaps roads will have to be widened to carry increased traffic. Additionally, the jobs offered in these operations are likely to attract new workers. If these workers are of child-bearing age, their arrival might require the town to plan not only for a variety of housing, but perhaps even consider enlarging schools and playgrounds. New subdivisions might have to be built, new shopping centers allowed, and more public parks provided. Conversely, if projections show a loss of industrial plants, the town might expect its younger workers to leave in search of suitable jobs elsewhere, leaving the town a place populated by more elderly individuals with needs for small apartments, ample public transportation, and perhaps a greater number of nursing homes. The point is, the effects of economic activity on a town's population determine the parameters of how land must be used.

There are other determinants of land use as well. State governments, and the federal government too, make many decisions that affect land within municipal boundaries. The state might route a new highway through a town, the Federal Aviation Administration may enlarge a nearby airport, or the U.S. Defense Department might close an adjacent army base. Any such decision would change a town's economic life and the way land might get used there. A town's plan, therefore, tries to measure the intentions of all external bodies that can affect the town's circumstances.

And finally, a plan expresses and details townspeople's wishes for the future. These wishes might be small matters, such as streets that have more shade trees planted along them. Or, they might be complex, such as attracting a wider assortment of manufacturing firms so as to make citizens' fortunes less dependent on the economic health of a single industry. The premise of governmental control over land use is that these goals can best be realized if they are the basis for evaulating individual proposals to develop land.

Together, these facts, opinions, projections, and communal hopes for the future fashion a comprehensive plan. Although years of professional activity have been devoted to innovations in the essential form of the comprehensive plan, its most familiar representation remains the original one: a map which depicts a community's intentions for the future by designating how undeveloped land should be used. This map will indicate, for example, where new residential, commercial, and industrial uses will be allowed; where new public facilities will be sited; and where roads will be built or widened. In effect, the plan states how land within the town's boundaries will accommodate changes in housing needs, employment opportunities, educational requirements, and transportation over a period of about 20 years.

The plan includes a clear definition of how growth should be guided so as to avoid the mistakes citizens feel were caused by past land use decisions. Not surprisingly, given the complex mix of human wishes and opinions that exist in any town, and the various personal circumstances and economic realities there, drawing up a plan is a complicated matter. The hopes and wishes of one group in the town might contradict others; certain types of economic growth may seem desirable to one faction and inconceivable to others. For these reasons, the preparation of a comprehensive plan is aided, typically, by professional planners whose expertise can help find a consensus of community opinion and translate a municipality's goals for its future into documents for guiding growth efficiently. Planners are trained to consider the full range of effects that particular land use choices will occasion—the traffic that will be generated, the schools that will be needed, the necessity for parks, and so on. Because of this analysis, they can evaluate alternative ideas for development and give sound guidance as a town tries to imagine a better future.

The planning staff submits a draft of the plan to the planning commission, which then holds a public hearing. Based on testimony there, the commission may or may not amend the plan, may or may not direct the staff to draft additional editions of the document, may or may not hold supplementary public hearings, but eventually will agree on a single best version of the comprehensive plan and forward it to elected leaders with a recommendation for adoption. The local governing body will read the plan and transcripts of the planning commission's hearing, hold its own hearing, and ultimately adopt a comprehensive plan for the jurisdiction.

No matter the process used or the difficulty of gathering necessary facts and opinions and finding a consensus on appropriate civic goals, the harmonious result the state intends is an adopted comprehensive plan. Once adopted, the comprehensive plan becomes the source of legitimacy for planners' recommendations about how development should occur. Arguments planners might make for orderly development, for where new capital facilities should be sited, for what the town expects from future development, even for recommendations on mundane matters of construction, all flow from this comprehensive statement of a town's goals for itself.

Paradigmatic Step 2: Land Use Regulations. Once the plan is adopted, local elected leaders implement it by formulating ordinances and policies. Again, these officials rely on the planning staff to draft these policies and on the planning board to hold a public hearing before making formal recommendations of adoption. Finally, the local governing body will adopt and codify the land use regulations as ordinances or formally adopted policies, and turn their administration over to the planning staff.

Planners have been trained to work with several tools for seeing that the plan becomes reality. They know principles of planning for capital facilities: how land uses are likely to change because of a new roadway or sewer line. They have learned such community development skills as how to rehabilitate failing neighborhoods and bring new life to derelict commercial areas. They can coordinate and review policies undertaken by other agencies of local government. For example, planners ensure that decisions made by the city street department complement the comprehensive plan.

Yet, of all the skills and authorities planners use to see a plan realized, land use regulations are the most powerful. The most commonly used are zoning ordinances, subdivision regulations, and review of construction plans.

[Zoning Ordinances]   At their simplest, zoning ordinances delineate the precise areas, or zones, where houses can be built, as distinguished from where commercial and industrial enterprises can exist. The earliest use of zoning was simply to prevent one type of activity from becoming a nuisance to another. The smell of an abattoir, for example, was kept from offending homeowners by stipulating that slaughterhouses would not be allowed near residential districts. When zoning is first undertaken in a town, boundaries for districts are usually drawn around existing areas known by their predominant uses, and the ordinance specifies that new construction within each district be limited to buildings similar to those already there.

Gradually, individual zoning ordinances become more complicated as elected officials make new stipulations either to prevent mistakes or to encourage pleasing construction. For example, residents in areas zoned for apartment buildings might complain that they have inadequate parking spaces. In response, the governing body may amend the zoning requirements to require a standard number of offstreet parking spaces for each housing unit. Or, residents may think tourists will find the town more attractive if commercial enterprises were landscaped, and as a consequence ask their elected officials to make this a requirement of business zones.

At their most complex, zoning ordinances codify all the particulars of appropriate development as specified in the comprehensive plan. They divide municipal territory into zones or districts and designate conditions of construction within each. Each district typically has an authorized limit on the size of a building parcel; on size, height, and placement of structures on a lot; and on the number of parking spaces required. And each zone specifies the uses to which buildings and land in the district can be put. Zoning ordinances can also specify smaller details of lot development that the comprehensive plan envisions. Citizens might agree that a certain desirable grace results from houses being placed back from the street at a uniform distance. Such an aesthetic can be articulated in their comprehensive plan and realized by specifying a mandatory front-yard depth that builders of new houses must provide.

Since developers must obtain official certification from a town that their proposals comply with all legislated restrictions on their parcels, zoning ordinances are powerful mechanisms for implementing a comprehensive plan. Somewhat tempering this power are the provisions for making amendments to zoning ordinances, and for flexible or individualized treatment of particular parcels within a district. Zoning districts can be changed, as noted above, by using a process probably now familiar to the reader: proposals to change the zoning ordinance by redrawing its boundaries or altering its requirements are evaluated by the planning staff, and presented with a recommendation for action to the planning board. The board conducts a public hearing and makes a recommendation to the governing body, which holds another public hearing and ultimately decides whether or not the ordinance needs amendment. If enacted, such a change would affect all new construction that occurs on any parcel within the zone.

A change in the zoning requirements for individual parcels can also be made, through a somewhat different process. Cities and counties have citizen boards of adjustment which are authorized to grant a variance from the terms of a zoning ordinance where literal enforcement would result in unnecessary hardship to a landowner. For example, a certain residential zone might require at least a 10-foot separation between a house and any property line that defines the lot on which it would be built. Due to irregular topography, however, there might exist a legally recorded lot only 30 feet wide which perhaps lies between a city street and a meandering creek. Strict enforcement of the zoning ordinance would mean that a house could only be 10 feet wide, or that nothing at all could be built there; but, in either case, a clear economic hardship would be worked on the lot's owner. The board of adjustment will read the facts of such a situation, listen to the advice of the local planning staff, and conduct a public hearing on the matter before deciding whether a variance is warranted. In this hypothetical case, the board of adjustment would undoubtedly—and appropriately—grant a variance from the side-yard requirements for the single lot. Their decision is final, unless an aggrieved party appeals to the appropriate court of law. That is, a decision to grant a variance is informed by the planning staff, but is not heard by elected officials.

Zoning ordinances are predicated on the important assumption that an owner of land has the power to use or develop his land as he wishes except as specifically restricted in state and local legislation. These restrictions must be based on some definition of a public interest broader than the landowner's, and such an interest could be that stated in the comprehensive plan. In fact, since zoning first became a common method of controlling land use, most state zoning acts have contained the requirement that zoning be "in accordance with a comprehensive plan." Although planners read this phrase as requiring zoning ordinances to conform to a comprehensive plan prepared in advance of zoning ordinances, courts have only recently agreed. Earlier, most courts asked to review zoning ordinances generally found that comprehensive policies expressed in the ordinances themselves satisfied the statutory requirement; other courts required only that the data used to support land use decisions be rational and well thought out. And still other courts simply held that the traditional uses of zoning within a local jurisdiction comprised a comprehensive plan. Years of practice have made it clear that the police power of zoning is used more as a means to prohibit undesirable development than as a method to define and encourage desirable development which complies with the comprehensive plan.

The planning staff plays a central role in formulating and recommending new zoning ordinances, just as it does in drafting a comprehensive plan. Once the ordinances are adopted, the planning staff becomes their steward—explaining their requirements and rationales to the public, requiring compliance, and even monitoring their effectiveness and suggesting amendments.

Observations About What Americans Have Built

With little difficulty she located the brick gateposts that had once marked the service entrance of an estate she knew, and that now opened on the tract called Greenwood Acres. Of Barbara's house, which she had been to only twice, she remembered that it was on a street named for some shrub . . . In her numb mind lay images of a short driveway, a carport, a walk of round cement pads, an overturned tricycle, an entrance under a flat overhang, a vine climbing a wall . . . A street named for a shrub? They were all named for shrubs . . . The broken images upon which she had relied for recognition were worthless, for the driveway of each of these identical houses led to an invariable carport, and on every drive or sidewalk there seemed to be an overturned and forgotten tricycle . . . There was not a gas station, not a drugstore, from which to call—zoned out, she supposed, to keep holy the bedroom suburb.[8]

Wallace Stegner

[*Subdivision Regulations*]   Subdivision review is a time-honored means of regulating land development. The early purpose of subdivision regulations was to provide an efficient method of selling land. Owners drew maps showing their land divided into sequentially numbered blocks and lots. These drawings, known as *plats*, were recorded in an office of local government. Subsequent sales of land could then be made by reference to a recorded plat, rather than by a more cumbersome, and hence often erroneous, description in metes and bounds. Platting reduced costs and prevented conflicting deeds and also led to uniformity in survey methods. After World War II, quick residential growth came to most American towns, causing them to enact regulations which imposed conditions on subdividing land. To comply with the regulations, land developers shared in the costs of such residential necessities as public open space, parks, and adequate streets. Most recently, because municipal leaders have learned that the way land is divided and settled dictates future transportation networks, drainage patterns, and demand for public facilities, subdivision regulations take into account the relationship of a new subdivision to its external environment and to the community's comprehensive plan.

To be approved, proposed subdivisions must comply with locally adopted standards for common facilities such as roads. In addition, members of the community must be given an opportunity to comment on the proposal before it is approved. The purpose of the review process and the standards for development include promoting public health, safety, and general welfare; providing adequate light, air, and water; and harmonizing the needs of citizens with the natural environment. As with all planning ordinances, subdivision regulations are formulated by the planning staff, sometimes amended by the planning board after a public hearing, and formally adopted by the governing body. Subsequently, their administration lodges with the planning office.

[Review of Construction Plans] Before a developer can begin construction, he must obtain a permit to proceed, which certifies that the project conforms with all regulations having to do with development. The planning office usually takes responsibility for this last review, and it is in this capacity that planners can coordinate the relevant policies of various city or county departments. For example, the public works department has standards for street width and grade for all new roadways, and the planning department will not issue a permit without certification from the city engineer that proposed projects meet these standards. In turning over administration of its enacted ordinances to the planning office, a city or county acts on the reliance that when a building permit is issued, all applicable policies and ordinances have been satisfied.

Over time, land use ordinances accumulate, and regulations in effect are not necessarily those enacted by current elected officials. They are, however, an evolving record of a municipality's learning from experience and subsequently defining in legislative standards the kind of development that will be approved. The planning staff is responsible for keeping track of all ordinances that bear on developing land in any part of the local jurisdiction.

Paradigmatic Step 3: Development. It is when individual landowners decide to develop their property that a comprehensive plan can be realized. The precise timing of this development cannot be predicted, since only by using its power of eminent domain can government force the conversion of land. This power, which allows a government to buy privately owned land for public purposes, is limited by municipal finances and by American beliefs about the primacy of private ownership of land. Most governments, particularly local governments, simply do not have the cash to buy very much land, nor do they have popular support for using public funds for that purpose. These facts mean that only in rare instances do governments cause development; more usually their only active role is responding to a landowner's request for permission to build. Consequently, the comprehensive plan and land use regulations can take effect only as private decisions are made, at which time government can specify how such development is to occur.

Because private landowners only unpredictably decide to sell, much more land is designated for each type of use than would fulfill projections of need for that use. To designate less risks a shortage of necessary land and could inflate its price. Planning textbooks typically recommend a 25 percent overage be allowed,[9] but it's more common for towns to designate three or even four times as much land for, say, residential purposes, than would be required in the foreseeable future. This necessarily means that some scattering of growth will occur, and that urban uses will spread somewhat haphazardly around the areas designated for future development. Eventually, though, if a town follows the state's paradigm for a rational sequence of planning, regulating, and developing land, local plans would be realized through an accumulation of private development decisions.

This brief discussion is meant to give the reader a sense of the state's idea of how land use decisions should be made and to show the broad outlines of the paradigm within which local government planners practice. However, development and land use decisions do not occur in isolation, but are simply one aspect of a town's or a county's day-to-day business.

Observations About What Americans Have Built

In stopping to take breath, I happened to glance up at the canyon wall. I wish I could tell you what I saw there, just *as* I saw it, on that first morning, through a veil of lightly falling snow. Far up above me, a thousand feet or so, set in a great cavern in the face of the cliff, I saw a little city of stone, asleep. It was as still as sculpture—and something like that. It all hung together, seemed to have a kind of composition: pale little houses of stone nestling close to one another, perched on top of each other, with flat roofs, narrow windows, straight walls, and in the middle of the group, a round tower.

It was beautifully proportioned, that tower, swelling out to a larger girth a little above the base, then growing slender again. There was something symmetrical and powerful about the swell of the masonry. The tower was the fine thing that held all the jumble of houses together and made them mean something.[10]

Willa Cather

Municipal Logic: Context of Land Use Decisions

States have set up local governments to finance and provide services with local consequence, such as police and fire protection, public schools, recreational activities, sewerage systems, local road mainte- nance, as well as land use planning. The more revenue elected leaders can collect, the greater versatility they will have to provide for their constituents' desires. And providing for those desires keeps local leaders in office. Depending on their state's enabling legislation, local jurisdic- tions can collect money from such sources as income or sales taxes; however, their revenues principally come from a system of real property taxation which imposes levies on land and improvements—what has been built on the land—in direct proportion to market value. Conse- quently, the relationship between municipal revenues and the value of land is the pre-eminent fact of local government.

The precise value of land is no simple matter to determine, although there are some axioms well known to local officials. Value is obviously based in part on the actual market price of land and improvements. However, since how much is paid for land and how much is spent to erect a building on it are matters principally of private choice, public decisionmakers can exert little influence on these determinants of value. But value is also based on attributes of a property's location, and these are matters over which local leaders can exert considerable discretion. Consider some familiar locational preferences. Industrial enterprises need access to outside markets, and therefore prefer to locate their operations near freeway interchanges or along railroad spurs. For the sake of convenience and diversion, families prefer to live close to public parks, schools, or shops carrying necessities of daily life; they also prefer to be distant from the noise and congestion of industry. Since local leaders choose where to build schools, where to provide parks, where industry can locate, and where houses can be built, they affect many of the consequential attributes that determine market value, and in this way affect property tax receipts.

Because local decisions affect the value of property, because local revenues come from taxes directly related to that value, and because the electorate judges the quality of its leaders by how reliably they can provide services without increasing levies, how land is used lies at the heart of municipal rationality. What this means is that as much as possible, local leaders make decisions about how land can be used within a logic containing two internally consistent propositions.

The first proposition is that a municipal budget must balance public service expenditures with revenues. This means that proposed developments are evaluated according to how much money they will bring into town, and how much they will cost. Taxable value of a development determines revenues, and the public services required there determine costs. Corporate headquarters, for example, carry a high valuation and make few demands for public services. They will be judged especially desirable, and even offered incentives such as temporary tax reductions to locate in a particular town. Conversely, towns don't want such developments as low-income housing because they cost more than they pay in taxes. In fact, municipalities will try to get the developer of such housing to pay for common facilities ordinarily financed by the local government. In short, a sophisticated municipality's interest in new development never strays far from the town's bottom line.

Municipal logic takes as its second propostion that property values should be maintained or enhanced. The town's interest here—a predictably high level of assessed valuation for property taxation—dovetails cleanly with the investment aspirations of landowners. Property owners who argue that a proposed mobile home park will cause a decline in the value of their property find elected leaders a sympathetic audience. The result is that towns find room for lower-valued projects at a remove from "better" uses, relying on physical separation to prevent property valuation from falling.

These two propositions go a long way in explaining how land use decisions are made: approvals are given to projects that serve the interests of municipal finance. Ideally, these interests would not conflict with the aims of land use planning. Logic would say that states must have intended harmony between towns' budgets and planning aims, since the power over each is specifically conferred by a state to its local jurisdictions.

A Beneficent Future

Local planning is authorized by enabling legislation which sees the municipal future as a pleasant extension of the present. In this view, people with the same background and similar expectations will influence patterns of development, and growth will eventually bring about a town's long-term goals. The pleasant paradigm is congruent with what people want to believe. Most civic leaders think that bad effects of growth—if they occur at all—can be remedied later with little loss to the common well-being. In the meantime, constituents can work the construction jobs that development brings, new businesses can open, and municipal tax receipts can fatten.

The state's beneficent paradigm for how land use decisions *should* be made does not accurately describe how these decisions *are* made. The reasons for this dichotomy are the subject of the next chapter.

NOTES

1. Fred Bosselman, "Reporter's Comment," *Land Use Law and Zoning Digest* 31 (January 1970): 22.

2. Bill Barich, *Laughing in the Hills* (New York: Penguin, 1981) p. 5.

3. *Planning Magazine* 53 (December 1987): 32.

4. F. Scott Fitzgerald, *The Great Gatsby* (New York: Charles Scribner's Sons, 1953), p. 23.

5. John L. Hancock, "Planners in the Changing American City, 1900-1940," *Journal of the American Institute of Planners*, 33 (September 1967): 293.

6. R. G. Tugwell, "Implementing the General Interest," *Public Administration Review*, (1940): 37.

7. James A. Spencer, "Planning Agency Management," in *The Practice of Local Government Planning* (Washington, D.C.: International City Management Association, 1979), pp. 68–73.

8. Wallace Stegner, *A Shooting Star*, (New York: Viking Press, 1961), pp. 88–90.

9. F. Stuart Chapin, Jr., and Edward J. Kaiser, *Urban Land Use Planning*, 3rd ed. (Champaign: University of Illinois Press, 1979), p. 408.

10. Willa Cather, *The Professor's House*, (New York: Alfred A. Knopf, 1964), p. 201.

2

Planners Marooned Where Public and Private Interests Meet

If towns grew and changed in the manner intended by state enabling legislation, a town-as-built would be the town that was planned. However, in most small American towns, comprehensive plans represent wishes not reflected in the planning department's definition of its mission, not represented in zoning ordinances and subdivision regulations, and not found in the physical environment. Sometimes this has happened for good reasons. No plan can precisely predict economic or demographic trends, nor can a plan foresee fundamental changes in popular preferences or leisure time activities. Certainly few plans forecast technological breakthroughs that make previous planning assumptions obsolete. Any of these changes to a town's situation should and can be accommodated either by amending the comprehensive plan and any relevant land use regulations, or by interpreting legislated provisions in light of new events. Indeed, if such changes could not be accommodated, plans would enforce a rigid adherence to an outdated understanding of municipal characteristics and expectations. By remaining static, plans would impede beneficial development.

However, many towns allow changes to their comprehensive plans and approve construction of particular projects not for reasons of public interest, but to promote an individual's private interests or to oblige a single neighborhood's wishes. This chapter will discuss how these bad land use decisions and inappropriate developments occur despite the ideal paradigm for guiding growth. It will also show how such decisions ignore local government planners' advice about how a community should grow. The point of the discussion will not be to lament a commonplace situation, but to find points of intervention where planners could rejoin the planning process and make stronger arguments for good land use decisions. The chapter will end by introducing *committed lands analysis*, a method which offers planners a new option for expressing their point of view. The method is useful because it is based on the way planners must understand their role in the actual process of land use decisionmaking.

Observations About What Americans Have Built

. . . He wanted to know why the dam was being built, and I said I didn't know, but of course I did. The dam would impound water to form an artificial lake, and the land around the lake would appreciate in value, and the realtors and developers would build the usual tacky resort facilities, and the people who made their fortunes by destroying things would be a little richer but not any safer from death. . . .

The next day I got some news from home. Out at the dam site "progress" was being made. The Corps of Engineers' bulldozers were working round the clock, plugging up nature with anal fervor, and we'd even had our first suicide, some poor young woman who'd jumped off the bridge that had been built over the basin to be dammed. Her freefall into dust and wild flowers struck me as a wholly appropriate symbol of a more general demise, of the specific sliding into the mass. The town's planning commission, chaired by a realtor, was busily amending the general plan, changing agricultural zoning to residential or commercial to accommodate the developers and carpetbaggers who were lining up along the avenues; on the plaza we now had a T-shirt store and a jewelry store and a store that sold candles, macrame, patchouli oil, incense, roach clips, and sensitive photographs of the very land parcels that were being rezoned. . . .[1]

Bill Barich

HOW LAND USE DECISIONS ACTUALLY GET MADE

States envision landowners' developing their property according to a town's plan and its land use regulations. However, if landowners or developers want to undertake something different, they can petition their local government to change applicable regulations or to waive specific requirements. These petitions are usually successful, particularly in the urban frontier and in other areas where there is not a well-organized neighborhood group. A comparison of actual development patterns and comprehensive plans in most cities would show that decisions ignored a broad community interest. As stable and steadfast as local land use plans and regulations might seem, they are either negotiable or impotent weapons against narrow sentiment. In fact, when making a decision about how to, or whether to, develop a particular property, developers do not consider regulations to be as important as bank interest rates, market surveys, or even building codes. The next few sections of this chapter will discuss why this is true, considering in turn the tools that have been given to towns and counties to guide the use of land, and the administrative structure authorized for local jurisdictions to make land use decisions.

Planning Tools: Guiding the Use of Land

States expect local jurisdictions to adopt a comprehensive plan, write land use ordinances for its implementation, and oversee the plan's becoming a reality as individuals develop their land. Under this paradigm, the plan represents a useful guide for future growth and contains an articulate and reliable description of what a town wants from the future. In practice, because citizens cannot easily agree on long-term goals—no matter how small and apparently homogeneous their town—local officials frequently adopt ambiguously phrased plans. Consider this as an ordinary example: "Land use policies should encourage beneficial development." Although such a goal appears in many plans, it can hardly provide guidance, since the word "beneficial" could seem to encourage residences, landfills, rendering plants, or airports, depending on one's private point of view. Developers designing a conforming project, and subsequently the planning board and elected officials charged to determine whether that proposed project complies with the comprehensive plan, must often resort to an ad hoc interpretion of "beneficial development." Their interpretations can easily be at variance not only with each other, but with what the larger community might believe.

The consequences are different in the urban frontier and in the urban protectorate. Few citizens will appear at public hearings regarding development decisions on the frontier because they usually can't see how their private lives would be affected. A wide range of views are not then available to guide decisionmakers, and the landowner or developer's desire to build a project is likely to prevail. In the urban protectorate, however, citizens *do* defend their neighborhood from any use they would rather not see, and their narrow, strongly held views are likely to persuade the decisionmakers to deny permission for controversial projects.

The public interest is thwarted in either case. On the frontier, a decision can get made that relies more on the persuasive powers of developers than on any reading of the community's wishes. And moreover, in the protectorate, a decision can get made that strengthens the status quo of politically adept neighborhoods and causes controversial projects either to go into less politically skilled areas of town or into the urban frontier.

Sketches of Planning Practice

A Reporter Satirizes the Urban Protectorate

Here are some questions and answers about the house of worship the Missoula Stake of the Church of Jesus Christ of Latter-day Saints (the Mormons) wanted to build in the West Rattlesnake but decided not to because of the opposition of some area residents (who appeared at several public hearings on the matter):

Q: Are West Rattlesnake residents who opposed the church building religious bigots?

A: Probably not, they just appear to be.

Q: Do Mormons erect attractive church buildings, enhance the landscape around them, maintain them, pay for them, and conduct admirable and wholesome activities inside them?

A: Yes, but so what? If you don't want Mormons in your neighborhood, you don't want Mormons in your neighborhood.

Q: Would Rattlesnake residents who opposed the church building also oppose a group home for developmentally disabled people?

A: Naturally. Developmentally disabled people, like Mormons, tend to create monumental traffic problems.

Q: Are the opponents liberal, open-minded and progressive?

A: Every last one of them—except when it comes to Mormons building a church in their neighborhood.

Q: Is there a chance opponents will regret that they didn't take advantage of an opportunity to acquire some friendly, stable neighbors?

A: Is the pope Catholic?[2]

The regulatory decisions that should carry out the comprehensive plan often override the community's wishes. If the comprehensive plan itself is vague, clear regulations for its implementation are more difficult to formulate. But even when plans are clearly written and unambiguous, towns adopt vaguely phrased land use ordinances. For example, when trying to describe land uses permitted within a district, zoning ordinances commonly use a phrase such as "compatible with adjacent uses." Unfortunately, while the word "compatible" is central to understanding the intention of the ordinance, it is vague and can reliably guide neither a developer trying to imagine a conforming project nor a public official trying to determine whether that project should be permitted in the zone. Land use regulations written in nebulous yet well-meaning prose create considerable interpretative discretion and promote development decisions that are capricious and arbitrary.

Even when planning goals and land use regulations are clearly written and unambiguous, there is often no apparent connection between the plan and its implementing policies. Many towns ignore the three-step paradigm of planning, regulation, and development described in Chapter 1. Instead, they adopt comprehensive plans but fail to enact policies for carrying them out. Other jurisdictions adopt zoning resolutions that merely codify existing land uses and contain only an accidental relationship with the comprehensive plan. But these misconnections between planning and implemention have not been understood as evidence of a town's ignoring its state's enabling legislation. Rather, courts have usually held that zoning measures need not be linked to a comprehensive plan. Towns have acted on these rulings and allowed plans to become no more than interesting anthropological finds showing how citizens once thought they would like their town to develop.

It is principally through interpretation of vague language in planning goals or land use ordinances that decisions are made contrary to a comprehensive plan's design. Incrementally, the plan becomes irrelevant to the way the town is actually being built. Because these contrary decisions are made so often, there should be some mechanism by which a plan can be modified to reflect changes—even bad changes—that come to a town. Consider a typical example. Swayed by a developer's argument that a proposed subdivision will serve valid public needs, a town zones for houses some land designated by the plan as open space. Such a decision should simultaneously consider the predictable needs of residential developments: children have to attend school and play, employed persons must commute to their jobs, and households need to buy groceries. Unfortunately, few towns look beyond the particular tract being rezoned. Their narrow vision undermines a comprehensive plan in this way: allowing the subdivision in designated open space may contradict one of the town's adopted goals, but failing to reconsider the appropriate use of contiguous tracts will contradict the plan's other goals. If local shopping areas are not nearby, people will have to make unnecessarily long automobile trips for their daily needs, thereby perhaps worsening air pollution problems that the plan intended to solve by reducing the necessity for numerous individual trips. The point to this example is that the planning process needs to respond to the ramifications of each decision, no matter how poor.

The sad fact is that as long as there has been local land use planning in America, there has been criticism that plans offer little useful direction for officials who must approve, deny, or modify requests for development approval. Plans don't even offer much assistance to developers trying to build in accordance with the town's desires. Most typically, plans are written in well-meaning prose, but become increasingly out-of-date with each subdivision built, each zoning district changed, and each variance granted. Citizens find the local planning staff unable to keep the plan flexible, unable to stop unsightly development in the urban frontier, and unable to argue for suitable projects in the urban protectorate. In fact, planners seem ill-equipped to perform the very jobs they were hired to do.

Sketches of Planning Practice

Two Developers' Regard for Land Use Regulations

Saturday, April 21, 1984. In a move that took city planning officials by surprise, ground was broken Friday in Missoula for what two men claim will be a half-mile, professional auto race track attracting drivers from throughout the United States and Canada. The developers say the facility will open June 10 with weekly professional stock-car racing throughout the summer. Located on 63 acres, the facility will seat 24,600 spectators.

But before construction can begin, the developers will need a city building permit, and the Missoula City-County Health Department will have to approve a sewage-disposal system. Missoula Planning Office Director Kristina Ford, whose office approves building projects, says she knew nothing of the racetrack until she was contacted by a Missoulian reporter at home Thursday night. The developers say they wanted to keep the wraps on the project until final details could be pulled together and they could announce the beginning of construction.

Tuesday, May 8, 1984. Developers of a proposed half-mile, professional stock-car race track on the outskirts of Missoula seem to be on a collision course with zoning and building regulations. Despite no exemption for paving the proposed parking lot and no building permits, the developers vowed Monday to forge ahead with the project. "We're going to build until a stop-work order is issued. . . . Further delays caused by the Missoula Planning Office will kill the project for this year."

A variance is necessary to avoid paving the parking lot. But a variance would have to come from the Missoula County Board of Adjustment and now can't be considered until its June 27th meeting. The developers say the first races must be held in June. The County planning staff counters that they gave enough notice to allow them to take the case to the board's May meeting, but the developers declined to apply.

"There's been no cooperation at all from local government. They don't want us to build it."[3]

Decisionmaking Structure for Land Use Decisions

While there are clear weaknesses in the tools of land use planning, a close look at the decisionmaking structure used in land use choices will reveal other reasons that a community's broad interests are ignored. Most states have given local governments a three-part administrative structure for managing growth and change. Elected leaders make decisions about the use of land by considering the advice of an independent planning board comprised of unelected laymen. The professional planning staff works for the board, bringing to its attention the matters which ultimately will inform the vote of the governing body. The staff performs all day-to-day duties relating to development. They explain the comprehensive plan, listen to complaints and answer questions about the requirements of various land use statutes. The planning staff ensures that projects satisfy the requirements for development that other municipal agencies impose, and issues building permits for approved projects.

Independent Planning Boards. As a fledgling profession, planning needed boosters and protectors in order to reach maturity, and planning boards surely did that. By now, however, state law provides planners the support once given by independent boards. Many states require their local jurisdictions to engage in planning; some going so far as to specify elements such as local housing needs or environmental concerns that must be addressed in the plan.[4] In addition, state courts have started to overturn municipal decisions made either in the absence of planning or without reference to a locally adopted plan.[5]

Boards now interpret comprehensive plans and land use regulations in light of broad community concerns. Board members are civically inspired, thoughtful citizens who bring to land use decisions an awareness of community attitudes and an appreciation of how individual decisions might interact. These personal attributes should allow them to interpret the comprehensive plan and land use regulations as municipal aspirations and conditions change. In addition, by holding public hearings the board can provoke a more thorough discussion of planning matters than the full agenda of locally elected officials would normally allow.[6] Land use decisions are typically made following two public hearings. The first is conducted by an independent planning board, and the second by local elected officials, who ultimately make a decision. Presumably, such a lengthy process ensures that all points of view regarding important land use matters will be heard and considered.

The usefulness of planning boards depends on two fundamental assumptions. First, that planning boards will act objectively when they choose among competing positions on a particular land use decision, when amending the comprehensive plan, or when suggesting new land use regulations to implement the plan. Second, that planning boards are well prepared to evaluate the arguments they will hear on land use matters, and will exercise good judgment in formulating a recommendation for action by the governing body. Throughout the country, practice belies these assumptions.

Planning boards do not act objectively. In fact, it is often economic self-interest rather than the public interest that draws people to serve on these boards, as their voting records bear out.[7] Alone, this fact wouldn't be so damning if all the economic interests in a town were represented on the board, but they are not. Real estate and development interests usually dominate the independent boards, and the recommendations made to elected leaders consequently represent their occupational bias regarding land use matters,[8] a bias which most often is in favor of development.

Observations About What Americans Have Built

A myth is a story told or an oft-told story referred to by label or allusion which *explains* a problem. . . . Very often, the problem being "solved" by a myth is a contradiction or a paradox, something which is beyond the power of reason or rational logic to resolve. . . .

The American has, does, will *adapt* civilization and wilderness to each other. In the mythic process of adaptation, the wilderness can be civilized, civilization can be improved, and the wilderness can be preserved; thus neither civilization nor wilderness is destroyed. All that is required are Americans who "believe that there is nothing they cannot accomplish, that solutions wait somewhere for all problems, like brides."[9]

James Oliver Robertson

Neither are planning boards well prepared to consider reliably the matters that come before them. Most board members have full-time jobs and, therefore, have inadequate time to read and think about staff reports which discuss items on the agenda. Consequently, the board's decisions are rarely fully informed, and in fact their advice can be systematically biased if the board becomes dominated by one or two diligent members who argue persuasively. These persuasive members are often people with a vested interest in growth, but they can also be residents from the urban protectorate intent on keeping the neighborhood free from unwanted uses. In either case, the advice the governing body receives from the planning board will not be objective responses to land use proposals.

Alternatively, once aware of the failings and inadequacies of the independent planning boards, elected officials might pay little attention to the advice the board gives.[10] But disregarding the board's advice is a costly way to manage the public's business, and it is costly to developers whose projects await the outcome of first the planning board's and then the elected officials' deliberations. For a developer to have proposed a project at all is probably to have invested capital in an engineering firm's drawings or in land options, and to wait is to incur opportunity costs on that capital; to wait for advice officials disregard is to incur opportunity costs for no reason. Ignoring the board's advice is costly to government itself: salaries are paid for the planning staff to prepare for two public hearings when, in fact, only one affects the ultimate decision. As well, public spirit turns to cynicism as citizens and planning board members watch professional efforts go for nothing. And finally, it is costly to the planning staff's standing in town. Through a common transference of blame, the planning staff comes to embody the faults of the needlessly lengthy two-hearing process of making land use decisions. The public views planners as the personification of bureaucratic red tape.

Some jurisdictions have tried to repair these deficiencies. To attract a more representative group of people to serve on the boards, as well as to encourage better preparation for meetings and better recommendations to elected officials, some towns pay salaries to their planning board members. Other municipalities have considered electing planning commissioners, hoping the prestige of holding an elected office will draw persons other than realtors and developers to serve on the board and simultaneously cultivate more thoughtful decisions.[11] Other towns believe that the underlying assumptions of the two-hearing process would be met if board members thought elected leaders would take their advice seriously. These cities have tried to strengthen the force of the board's recommendations by allowing them to be overruled only by a two-thirds vote of the governing body.[12] To reduce the amount of time developers spend in the two public hearings, some towns hold a single public hearing which both the planning board and the elected officials attend. Subsequently, the planning board makes a recommendation which the governing body considers in light of its own reactions to what was said at the joint hearing. The effect of these attempts to make planning boards act more objectively and responsibly has not been systematically studied, and neither has reform reached the great majority of towns.

Readers are certain to know exceptions to this summary. There are planning boards comprised of civic-minded individuals who strive to realize the broad community interest and make well-informed decisions. Such boards are unusual. In most towns, the discretion that planning boards exercise in interpreting land use documents, when combined with the narrow interests typically represented on the boards, have made the planning process irrelevant to development. This fact is not bothersome to most local governing bodies.

Local Governing Bodies. Once the planning board has voted its recommendation on a land use matter, the planning staff advertises a second public hearing to be held before elected officials (mayors, city council members, and county commissioners). At that hearing the staff will present its analysis of the decision to be made as well as the advice of the planning board. Then the public will be invited to speak to the matter. Finally, the local governing body will make a decision. This is the point at which the realities of local political life become clear—where short-term arguments persuade elected officials mindful of election dates.

Planners measure new development proposals by the extent to which public interests are satisfied: whether new housing will be appropriate for the community's needs; whether new businesses will create jobs suitable for residents; and whether new development will adversely affect traffic, air and water, erosion, or open space. However, these broad community concerns often seem remote, abstract, and even irrelevant to a politician trying to decide a development in dispute. Disputes arise over planning tools: over wording in the comprehensive plan, the meaning of requirements contained in land use ordinances, and the specific prerequisites to construction. For example, officials hear from a landowner who wants to develop a shopping center in an area the local plan designates as "low-density residential." The owner might remind leaders that he and the out-of-work construction crew he intends to employ are voting constituents; he might argue for his development in terms of increased tax revenue for the town and increased property values near his shopping center. And indeed he will be hard to deny. That the construction jobs are short lived and offer no lasting solution to unemployment problems; that another shopping center in a neighboring town might siphon off much of the hoped-for market strength, perhaps even causing the landowner to default on the taxes promised city officials; that the center will cause traffic problems on main routes leading to the site—all are typical of planners' concerns given little weight by elected officials in their land use decisionmaking.

Similarly, the governing body hears from a group opposed to an apartment building proposed in their neighborhood. The group might remind officials that they and their neighbors are voting constituents; they might argue that the apartment building will disrupt the peaceful harmony of their high-value part of town, perhaps even decreasing the total assessed valuation. They will probably propose that the developer build something other than apartments. A daycare center might be suggested, or an architect's office, or some other low-intensity enterprise that the neighborhood believes would be compatible with their private lives. And they, too, will be hard to deny. That there is little or no demand in town for the alternative uses they propose; that the apartment building is the only type of housing affordable by people currently living in substandard dwellings; that appropriate site design for the apartment building can in fact enhance the value of all contiguous sites; that not to develop the land wastes public assets provided to the tract at considerable public cost—all are arguments for development in the protectorate given little weight in local land use deliberations.

The antipathetic interplay between the logic of land use planning and the logic of municipalities occurs every day in countless city council chambers in every state, where the short-term, bottom-line view of local governing bodies overrides planners' professional and long-term view. The reality is that towns plan, regulate, and settle disruptes over development according to their sense of the municipal budget and local property values.

Equally important to land use decisions is the desire of elected officials to be reelected. Office holders cannot simply ignore a neighborhood's wish to be protected from undesirable uses. Nor can they ignore constituents who claim personal hardships have been caused by regulation of property. A newspaper in North Carolina put this fact in memorable terms:

> Anyone familiar with zoning procedures knows why it is difficult for local officials to protect broad public interests. A friend or customer comes before the local board, makes his request and explains that his livelihood depends on the approval of the request. If the board members do not comply, they have made an enemy for life—not one that lives in Raleigh, either, but one that lives close by.[13]

The simple fact is that when compliance with land use regulations is pitted against emotion, emotion will win.

This is the most benign understanding of the process by which land use plans and regulations are interpreted in ways sympathetic to individual landowners or single neighborhoods, but indifferent to a community's broader interests. Conflicts of interest in land use decisions and subornation of governmental officials are also commonplace— decisionmakers approve requests made by business associates, and payoffs go to officials for particular decisions. Each instance of this that comes to light is a fleeting scandal, and the ripple of public indignation too quickly disappears.

The reader may know of instances in which local governing bodies reach land use decisions by relying on the comprehensive plan and on the clear wording of local land use regulations. Certainly there are examples of towns that choose to spread typically objectionable land uses among all neighborhoods. But such instances are demonstrably rare. More frequent, although not widespread by any means, are attempts to force local governments to make the proper decision. Some states have specified what plans must include and have directed that the language of goals be unambiguous; other states have required that plans and land use regulations be coordinated. Available to local leaders is a vast quantity of planning literature devoted to describing innovations in plan-making and regulatory tools; and there are volumes of creative inventions suited for the unique circumstances of individual towns. Laudable and workable as they are, however, these ameliorative attempts are largely ignored because the short-term logic of local government officials and the discretion they wield overpowers attempts at reform.

Sketches of Planning Practice

A Case of Public and Private Interests Failing to Connect

In Montana, two legal methods can be used to divide land, the first being subdivision review in order to file a plat. A subdivision that will contain more than five lots must be reviewed by 25 local, state, and federal agencies; smaller subdivisions are reviewed by only five. To be approved, proposed developments must comply with locally adopted standards for common facilities such as roads, and public comment must be solicited. The purpose of the review process and the standards for development in Montana, as elsewhere, include promoting public health, safety, and general welfare; providing adequate light, air, and water; and harmonizing man's needs with the natural environment.

The second method of dividing land is exempt from the subdivision review process because Montana's legislature believes the lots so created will have insignificant public

effects. No review is required for lots at least 20 acres in size. Also exempt are transfers of land within a family, as well as the sale once-a-year of a parcel of any size. Divisions of land created by these exemptions are filed by using what are known as Certificates of Survey (referred to as COS, hereafter).[14]

The community's interest would be satisfied if the developments created by COS were no different from those created under the subdivision review process.[15] Unfortunately, this is not the case. In the absence of review by public agencies and of comment by citizens, tracts are so poorly designed that some have no legal access to public roads;[16] residents in unreviewed subdivisions often live with insufficient water for daily needs; there is no fire protection for lots outside the area served by rural fire departments; prime agricultural land converts to urban uses without public review; housing is created in areas perenially threatened by severe forest fire hazards; and roads are inaccessible to emergency vehicles on icy days. For all these reasons, unreviewed COS developments exemplify bad planning. In Missoula County, where there are 43,000 subdivided acres, 90 percent have been filed using the method of COS exemptions. An example shows how this can occur, using the case of a married man with two children, who owns 80 acres. Claiming the 20-acre exemption, he divides the tract into four parcels for himself and his family; each parcel is filed with a COS. Each family member can then sell a parcel of any size without review by using the occasional sale exemption. After selling a one-acre lot, the man's wife can choose to transfer part of her remaining 19 acres back to her husband, and another COS exemption can be filed; he can then use the occasional sale exemption to divide this parcel.

There is no time limit governing how long a person must hold a parcel before transferring title to part of it to a family member and filing a new COS. Clever use of the exemptions in Missoula has resulted in what are quite obviously subdivisions, but which have completely escaped subdivision review.

Of course, not all unreviewed subdivisions are built with intention to trick the local authorities. A few harsh winters may cause a rancher to sell an acre or two each year in order to pay his bills; nevertheless, after a few years, a development can exist which is essentially a subdivision, although it has been built slowly and has gone unreviewed. The public has an interest in this development just as it has an interest in platted subdivisions. In fact, the public subsidizes the profits the developers have made by avoiding review. As an example: 20 percent of Missoula County's road budget in 1980 was used to pave roads in four unreviewed developments.

The Local Planning Staff.   Local townscapes and the record of votes on land use matters show that planners, although hired to encourage an agreeable accommodation of growth and change, are often ignored. The commonplace view of planning that holds sway in small towns is lamentably easy to summarize. Developers see the local planning staff as functionaries whose irrelevant advice slows progress toward economic gain. Differently, but relatedly, elected leaders see planners as the problem children of local government who anger members of the public for reasons not obviously defendable. And even the proponents of planning in a community see the staff as ineffective against bad development. Ultimately, planners in small towns can come to see their role in local political life as quixotic. This is, however, a self-defeating attitude because it means planners do not expect their advice to be taken seriously. Planners become, then, less inventive in arguing for the public interest.

A consideration of the underlying reasons for these attitudes is essential to making local government planning a more dynamic part of growth and change in a town. Hostility to planning, misunderstanding of its goals, and ineffective support together explain why planners are in effect excluded from the actual process of making land use decisions.

[Hostility to Planning] Among Americans there is only a grudging acknowledgment that planning is needed at all. A few visionary officials warn about the perils of uncontrolled change, but to most of their constituents these fears seem out of proportion to what exists: perhaps a few vacation houses appearing on a lakefront or a new gasoline station standing in an open field. Most civic leaders believe that the bad effects of growth—if they occur at all—can be remedied later with little loss to the common well-being. Following this logic, today's land use decisions in most small towns resemble the politics of the American frontier:

> Given the cornucopia of the frontier, an unpolluted environment, and a rapidly developing technology, American politics could afford to be a more or less amicable squabble over the division of the spoils, with the government stepping in only when the free-for-all pursuit of wealth got out of hand. In the new era of scarcity, laissez-faire and the inalienable right of the individual to get as much as he can are prescriptions for disaster. It follows that the political system inherited from our forefathers is moribund.[17]

Few citizens believe the political system is moribund. Most citizens and the officials they elect find it hard to believe that growth—usually meaning the modest construction activities of fellow townspeople—could be consequential enough to require governmental guidance. A history of slow growth confirms this attitude. Many small towns have in a sense *accumulated* over the years: a small entrepreneur will construct a factory; if it becomes profitable, a local contractor will build a house for the factory owner, and after a year or so, apartments for workers; later still, perhaps a coffee shop will open. In towns like this, a laissez-faire growth management technique seems adequate, and planners can successfully be represented as unnecessary—or worse, as obstructors of prosperity.

Furthermore, while it makes good administrative sense to have planners the stewards of the comprehensive plan and land use regulations, the effect of this stewardship is to make planners seem like scolds. They seem continually to be reminding elected officials of the rules of development, when, in fact, these rules were enacted by previous elected officials for reasons lost to the city's archives. Elected officials, too, can feel hostility to the planning staff, whom they see as hindrances to fresh methods of guiding a town's growth.

City council and county commission members also find that planning often argues its points in terms that are vague or complicated. Developers, on the other hand, make easily followed arguments: they claim proposed projects will mean new tax revenue and new jobs. Proper consideration would require calculation both of public revenues and of increased public service costs engendered by the project—the type of analysis planners are trained to make. But because many leaders neither understand nor take an interest in such analysis, they are reluctant to side with the planning department's expertise when it is contrary to the developer's assertion. Consequently, developers' promises of municipal benefit go unchallenged, and their projects are approved based on their own optimistic but poorly informed computation of public benefits and costs. However, once the developments have been built, towns have often had to impose new tax levies to correct developers' faulty computations of revenue and public service costs. Planners' early warnings of this result will enhance their reputation as municipal scolds, but probably not win allies.

Sketches of Planning Practice

Hostility to Planning—A Series of Letters

Cut the Punks

Why should we cut the sheriff's staff in the face of an outsized crime rate? There must be at least a dozen useless punks on the planning and zoning boards whose only function is to soak up the budget and socialize privately owned, taxable property.

Really Very Simple

To the city-county officials: the financial problems you are facing are not as large as they seem to be. It is really very simple!

. . . The planning board has a huge excess of employees, which is absolutely and unequivocally too much drain on the over-burdened taxpayer who is struggling to make ends meet and place food on the table.

Deputies Needed

I think it would be tragic to cut 15 from the sheriff's department. We need every deputy we have. . . . Why not economize by cutting nonessential services like the planning department? . . . The planning department is simply causing controversy amongst the residents. It encourages people with pet peeves to draft regulations to further strangle the economy. We have too many rules and regulations now.[18]

[Misunderstanding of Planning's Goals] By the very term *comprehensive planning*, the profession seems overcomplicated to most people. Many citizens, in fact, take the term to imply that the local planning staff is busily engaged in imposing its own vision of the future on the community. Reading the comprehensive plan is a formidable task to almost anyone. It is long, based on a great compendium of data and information, devised by complex technical methods, and too often written in professional jargon. For most citizens, it seems futile to attempt to understand what the plan contains and how the plan leads planners to make the suggestions they do. As a consequence, many people dismiss the plan, and consider planners as mysterious bureaucrats foisted on them. Some people are even skeptical of the planners' motives:

> It is always sobering to encounter the intellectual idealists at work, for they seem to live in a realm of their own, making plans for the world in much the same way that any common tyrant does.[19]

Alternatively, citizens will seize on a particular planning precept out of context. Take as an example the familiar notion of "preserving neighborhood character." Planners know that this goal—laudable as it is—has to be balanced with other community considerations, such as achieving equal opportunity in housing options for all income classes. In fact, while the meaning of the phrase "preserving neighborhood character" seems intuitively obvious, it actually engages some of the most complicated professional considerations that planners learn. However, in the urban protectorate this notion has been summoned in defense of blatantly exclusionary land use decisions.

Planners are also blamed for what they believe is one of their virtues: coordinating and explaining all regulations related to land that must be satisfied before a building permit can be issued. Planners explain the fire department's requirements for road widths, the city engineer's standards for paving roads, and the health department's rules about acceptable water supplies. Citizens often do not recognize that many of these requirements are not planning ordinances, and lodge complaints against planning that really should be directed against another department. For practical political reasons, however, elected officials probably will not correct an angry constituent's perception that it is the planning department holding up a building permit. Constituents come to their leaders for sympathy, not a lecture in civics. The coordinative function of planners creates the misunderstanding that they wield too much power over individual developers, an attitude that elected leaders sponsor by agreeing or by not correcting misapprehensions.

Sketches of Planning Practice

Hostility to Planning

"You might as well let him run the whole city. He's got more power now than the President of the United States," a city council member said, referring to the planning director of a small California community.[20]

[Ineffective Support for the Planning Office]   For two reasons, citizens ordinarily do not think of themselves as beneficiaries of the planning process and are not much moved to appear in public hearings as planners' allies. First, planning is characteristically invisible when it is most successful. Good planning avoids problems, anticipates and solves difficulties, and enables traffic to move smoothly through commercial districts. These are all virtues unnoticed by most citizens. Second, planners often argue on behalf of residents who do not yet exist. When the planning staff undertakes negotiations with developers about a community water system or sidewalks, or even playgrounds within the development, the beneficiaries of those negotiations are members of the "market" who ultimately buy lots. Most people who move into the subdivision take for granted whatever amenities exist, unaware that the planning staff was their partisan.

Observations About What Americans Have Built

I love my country's government for its attempt, in a precarious world, to sustain a peaceful order in which work can be done and happiness can be pursued not for the good of the state, but in a state that exists for our good. I love my government not least for the extent to which it leaves me alone.[21]

John Updike

Furthermore, a town's residents rarely want to be bothered with the day-to-day mechanics of city hall or the county courthouse. Most citizens want local government invisible and reliable, and ask only that it provide an untroubled atmosphere in which private life can flourish. Popular support of planning usually appears as short lived enthusiasms —for walkways along a park, for preservation of an old train station, or for preventing a car dealership from being sited beside a picturesque farm. In contrast, the development community's pursuit of approval for its projects takes the form of well-rehearsed arguments which, rather than addressing the concerns planners might have raised, commend its proposals as essential to a local government's ability to encourage economic opportunity, increase employment, or sweeten property tax receipts. Because of this, planners' advice often seems to stand alone, to be trivial compared to government's larger concerns, or to represent a position backed only by uninformed partisans.

The public's frail support for planning further erodes when approved developments are obviously at odds with the goals of their comprehensive plan. Citizens look around and see subdivisions where there was to have been open space, or they notice a shopping mall drawing business from the downtown shops the town had ostensibly agreed should be supported. A feeling grows, not of apathy, but of capitulation to the inevitability of bad land use decisions. To the citizenry, the planning office comes to seem ineffectual at best, unnecessary at worst. To come to their support at a public hearing seems embarrassing or a waste of time.

Sketches of Planning Practice

A Small Tale of Public Support for Planning

When a wildlife habitat becomes a rustic subdivision, often a real estate agent has greased the machinery of progress. But one Missoula, Montana, firm is working to preserve the land it sells.

Eco Realty was started in 1972 by broker Paul Brunner after he was harassed by local industry members for advocating land use planning in a talk at the University of Montana. "I was selling a lot of houses but was fired, and my boss told me I wasn't going to work again in the area," Brunner says. "I was blacklisted. The board of realtors filed charges of unethical conduct against me. It was funny in a macabre way.[22]

[The Ultimate Effect on the Planning Office]   Hostility to planning, misunderstanding of its aims, and the absence of effective support help explain the fact that bad land use decisions continue to be made. The persistence of these bad decisions—and worse, their long-lasting physical results—demoralizes planners so that they come to see all developers, landowners, realtors, and bankers as opponents. By incorrectly polarizing the positions of planners and the development community, this hostile attitude defeats the aims of the planning profession. It means that developers and planners—the people with the most training and practical experience with land—don't talk to each other in the early stages of a project, when each side could enlighten the other without much time or money being lost.

Instead, because of their mutual antagonism, planners and developers meet professionally only when a completely drafted proposal is submitted for review. Developers at this stage are predisposed to resist criticism, no matter how constructive, because of the high costs of making changes to their blueprints. For their part, planners have little time to offer suggestions for a better design, since most land use regulations restrict the period of time such a review can take. The money already spent on submitting the proposal and the deadlines imposed on planners' review effectively preclude creative suggestions from being proposed or taken seriously. This means that if planners find flaws in a developer's proposal, an already adversarial relationship worsens. Developers see planners as bureaucratic obstructionists ignorant of private enterprise's economic realities; planners see developers as high-handed opportunists unconcerned about their community's well-being.

Everyone loses here. Lost is the opportunity for conceiving development projects that respond both to public and private concerns. Lost is the chance to exchange professional ideas for innovative and efficient designs. And lost also is the disarming possibility that cooperation between private interests and planners could form a well-planned community and more—an effective constituency for good land use decisions.

The fact is that local government planning practice comes to be marooned. Developers choose not to consult with planners, preferring to take their chances with elected officials, who ignore planners' unpopular advice. Many planners who realize that they are not important advisors to land use decisions unfortunately become uninventive. Of course, such an attitude is self-defeating because uninspired arguments are easily countered and dismissed. Experience at the local level concludes that planning has to regenerate itself each time it asks to be taken seriously. Planners must not only argue their pertinence, but do so in the face of antagonism from developers, elected leaders, and the public whom planners are meant to serve.

The reader is sure to know of exceptions, but they are infrequent or not long-lasting. The practice of local government planning discourages many planners. Some quit fighting for better results, while others quit the profession altogether.

The Final Result: Bad Land Use Decisions

When planning staffs are weak, bad land use decisions are the result. There are many definitions of bad land use decisions, and people working to improve planning practice must choose what they think are most important. The definition used in this book arises from these prior formulations: while established neighborhoods prevent development on available tracts, undesirable uses go to the politically weak sectors of town and new construction sprawls across an ever-enlarging urban frontier. The reforms that this book proposes mean to help prevent these bad land use decisions.

The preceding discussion of the decisionmaking structure for land use is not news. As long ago as 1963, a study group of the American Law Institute wrote:

> The present legal framework for decisionmaking in the field of land use planning and regulation remains a product of the twenties, notwithstanding a mass of encrustations. . . . This framework not only fails to further the accomplishment of reasonable planning goals but its use is often incompatible with the functioning of the democratic process. This system . . . in many instances fails to recognize and protect valid local needs.[23]

But it is not the authors' intention to belabor the lamentable logic by which certain areas of towns are protected, others become dumping grounds, and the urban frontier spreads. Planners and most interested citizens certainly know this logic firsthand—have, in fact, known it for years—although their knowledge has generally not translated into changes to the decisionmaking process nor its internal logic. They continue to see what Henry James saw after a 20-year absence late in the nineteenth century: ". . . a land plundered but showing no sign of replacing ravage by civilization."[24]

There have been many innovations in the tools planners use and in the administrative structure by which land use decisions get made. They are good ideas, refreshed with each new edition of professional planning journals. But still, land use decisions get made in public hearings at which planners and developers are adversaries. Developers at this point represent themselves as entrepreneurs who will bring new jobs and new tax revenues; they represent planners as a narrow-minded staff unable to see beyond the letter of the law. For reasons described earlier in this chapter, local officials are inclined to agree and to vote with the developers.

Only two changes will allow good decisions to be made in such a forum and will offset the emotion that always beats the planning staff's dry logic. First, new arguments, well made and easy to understand, will get serious attention from elected officials. Second, if planners and developers were to work together long before appearing at the public hearing, the development proposal as finally presented could benefit the whole community. Planners will serve their community best if they put their expertise to work in helping design projects that comply with the comprehensive plan, rather than making ineffective objections to a proposal at a time elected leaders are disposed to approve the development.

What appears in the remainder of this book is a new way to argue for good development. It offers a method to be used by developers at the time they first begin to conceive projects, so that planners and developers can work together to find the best future for their town or county. This book is intended for citizens interested in better land use decisions, citizens who have been frustrated by the inability of their own arguments, and those of their local planning staff, to persuade elected officials.

COMMITTED LANDS

Bringing Planners Back into Land Use Decisions

The following three chapters describe a project conceived by the authors in Montana in 1986. It was a year of fiscal distress—distress caused by revenues falling 13 percent short of expected receipts. Furthermore, the state had estimated that its budget for the next two years would show a similar deficit. In response, budgets were pared, services reduced, and public attention focused almost exclusively on the revenue side of Montana's fiscal dilemma—a perspective that was understandable for at least two good reasons. First, the problem seemed to be with revenues, and so it seemed logical that solutions be sought there. Second, many expenditures simply could not be reduced in the short term, and given the current urgency it seemed fruitless to analyze them. These responses were typical of many states, and many local governments in the country that year and the years thereafter. While the particulars of the fiscal distress in Montana may differ from those in other states, the project described here will apply wherever fiscal difficulties beset towns and counties with few options for finding new revenues.

This project originated in the certainty that close attention to governmental budgets could be as useful for relieving fiscal problems as finding new revenues. Clearly, many seemingly nondiscretionary expenditures occur because leaders give approval to development proposals. As an illustration, consider the costs of building and maintaining local infrastructure—with infrastructure broadly defined here to mean both capital facilities such as roadways, and common public services such as street maintenance. Approving a subdivision project located beyond existing services predictably creates new infrastructure needs which, in time, can cost government more than the sum of additional tax revenues paid by that project's residents. New capital facilities may have to be built despite excess capacity elsewhere. Fire and police protection, school busing, snow clearing, and road maintenance—all these have to be provided, and each item carries costs related directly to the project's distance from town.

In Montana, where per capita mileage of locally financed roads ranks third in the nation and distances between settlements within single counties are often great, costs related to location can be substantial. Because Montana has allowed development to be scattered, infrastructure is expensive: per capita spending on public schools ranked fourth in the nation in 1984, and the state spent nearly twice the nation's per capita average on highways. Furthermore, local sewerage systems and drinking water facilities are generally in poor condition because they are overextended, both financially and spatially. In many localities, it's clear that even a small amount of additional development, if not properly guided, will have devastating effects on fragile public systems.

Montana can, of course, find ways to reduce some of its infrastructure costs: by consolidating school districts, for example, or by sharing the costs of equipment among jurisdictions. Yet, an expansive pattern of development commits local governments to an array of service demands whose expense cannot quickly be reduced. However, if future growth could be clustered within existing service districts, average public costs could eventually be reduced. In every county in the state, snowplows clear roads through undeveloped lands to reach distant settlements; school buses drive long miles to pick up only a few children. Clearly, encouraging or focusing development in carefully chosen portions of this in-between land—keeping in mind the particular community's needs and desires for open space—could increase the efficiency of any infrastructure wherein excess capacity exists. Inasmuch as the community has committed itself to providing services there, the phrase *committed lands* describes the vacant tracts that lie within governmental service districts. If growth could be directed to these lands, rather than be allowed to spread where new infrastructure would have to be extended at public cost, delivery systems could be made more efficient, capital facilities requirements could be lessened, and per capita costs reduced. Finding ways to achieve these goals would be sensible at any time, but it is especially crucial where a state's ability to help finance local governments has so considerably declined.

The method to be suggested was devised in Montana, but it can be used to argue for better land use decisions in towns of all sizes and in states everywhere. *Committed lands analysis* intends exactly this: to help make a good case for guiding growth into lands where public investments have been made. Often times such lands as these are in the urban protectorate—places where planners and rational observers of infrastructure and government finance know that future development should go. Committed lands analysis offers planners some control over the dynamics of growth in these areas. The analysis provides a new form of argument for changing plans and land use regulations in response to citizens' preferences and to the imperatives of local government finance. It can even offer a way to make the best of past bad land use decisions and to raise the esteem of planners in the minds of elected officials and the public.

The first principle of committed lands analysis is that development patterns are determined by an interplay among public and private parties—for example among county commissioners, directors of public works, landowners, and private developers. For this reason, a system devised to guide growth can succeed best if it is interjected into the decisionmaking processes of all these people whose actions affect land development. The project's abiding aim has been to engage all parties to development decisions.

Throughout America, local governments have traditionally approved development proposals under the assumption that growth anywhere means increased tax revenues. This attitude has been particularly influential when development proposals occur following a period of economic pessimism and decline. But as a consequence of this enthusiasm, there has been little scrutiny of the costs which development incurs. Evidence of over-eager approval of development is apparent in nearly every small, relatively slowly growing town in America. Successful projects scatter at excessive public expense across the landscape, but unsuccessful developments have also proven costly. Bankrupt developers, for instance, have defaulted on the loans local governments made to help install necessary public improvements, and taxpayers bear the costs of repaying the defaulted loans and of providing services to those citizens who moved in before the project was abandoned. The point is that future decisions to allow development must be made so that the costs of local infrastructure can be reduced as growth occurs.

The analyses performed in this project are similar to the methods many American municipalities use in order to impose impact fees on developers. These fees are meant to pay for the infrastructure that new projects require—for sewers, roads, sidewalks, utilities, among others, and the cost of maintaining them. If a developer chooses a site already provided with these basic support systems—a *committed tract*, in the project's conception—a smaller, or possibly no impact fee, would be required. After reading this book, perhaps some local governments will choose to impose impact fees. But given the traditional attitudes toward growth in small towns, that choice seems highly unlikely and may not even be desirable. However, we seek the same effect that such fees cause, namely that the public costs associated with private development are considered before a particular project site is chosen. If this happens, and if developers are encouraged to choose sites in *committed lands*, growth can increase infrastructure efficiency.

At its heart, committed lands analysis has an eminently practical purpose. One lesson that can be learned from periods of economic downturn is that many traditional methods of making development decisions need to be reexamined. The urgent fiscal problems of small towns across the country have created a public atmosphere receptive to ideas that could help states solve their financial problems and prevent their recurrence. The aim of this project is to show decisionmakers how to use growth to reduce public costs. Before, analysis such as suggested here might have been dismissed as unnecessary, or else accused of arising from aesthetic revulsion to sprawl, or even maligned as being antibusiness. It is none of these, and, in all probability, it will not seem so now.

Committed lands analysis is a fresh way to conceptualize an old problem, based on full consideration of the ways that bad land use decisions get made both in the urban frontier and protectorate. The methods can easily be adapted to the specific circumstances of particular jurisdictions. The ideas can be developed further, and the underlying analysis of why planning is weak in small towns can be used to strengthen the planner's point of view in other ways. Committed lands analysis is described here in a spirit of experimentation.

NOTES

1. Bill Barich, *Laughing in the Hills* (New York: Penguin, 1981), pp. 29 and 145.

2. Column by Steve Smith, "Missoulian," June 25, 1983, p. 6.

3. "Missoulian," April 21, 1984, and May 8, 1984, p. 6 and p. 8.

4. Daniel R. Mandelker and Edith Netter, "Comprehensive Plans and the Law," in *Land Use Law: Issues for the Eighties* (Chicago: American Planning Association, 1981), pp. 77-84.

5. Mandelker and Netter, "Comprehensive Plans," pp. 55-75.

6. *Matthews Municipal Ordinances* (2d ed.), 8A.01-8A.03.

7. Marion Clawson and Harvey S. Perloff, "Urban Land Policy: Alternatives for the Future," in *Management and Control of Growth*, vol. 3 Randall W. Scott, ed. (Washington, D.C.: The Urban Land Institute, 1975), pp. 10–11.

8. Even though elected leaders appoint planning board members, they must choose among a pool of volunteers; it is in this pool that real estate and development interests are disproportionately represented.

9. James Oliver Robertson, *American Myth, American Reality* (New York: Hill and Wang Publishers, 1980), pp. 6 and 44.

10. These points have been made by various critics. Robert A. Walker wrote the first thorough criticism of independent planning boards and commissions in 1941, in *The Planning Function in Urban Government* (Chicago: University of Chicago Press); a second edition of this book was published in 1950. Other notable works include: John T. Howard, "In Defense of Planning Commissions," *Journal of the American Institute of Planners*, **17** (Spring 1951); Frederic N. Cleaveland, "Organization and Administration of Local Planning Agencies," in *Local Planning Administration*, Mary McLean, ed. (Chicago: International City Managers' Association, 1959); David W. Craig, "A Plea for the Eventual Abolition of Planning Boards," *Planning 1963* (Chicago: American Society of Planning Officials, 1963); B. Douglas Harman, "City Planning Agencies: Organization, Staffing, and Function," *Municipal Yearbook 1972* (Washington, D.C.: International City Management Association, 1972).

11. "For the Record: Planning Commissioners Speak Out," *Planning Magazine* **50** (August 1984): 6.

12. "For the Record," p.6.

13. Robert G. Healy, *Land Use and the States,* (Baltimore: Johns Hopkins University Press, 1976), p. 9.

14. Title 76, Chapter 3, *Montana Codes Annotated.* The reasoning here is that people who are not land developers may transfer land to family members as a way of planning their estates, and that landowners occasionally need money from a land sale. The effects of a few such transactions per year would not substantially affect the larger public.

15. Of course, the developers who submit proposals to subdivision review would be penalized by suffering opportunity costs during the time the review process takes.

16. Minutes of the meeting on March 16, 1983, of the Agriculture, Livestock, and Irrigation Committee of the Montana State Senate, Exhibit 4.

17. William Ophuls, "The Scarcity Society," *Harper's Magazine* (April 1974): 26–31.

18. The letters appeared in the "Missoulian" on June 12, 1983; June 21, 1983; and May 24, 1983.

19. E. B. White, as quoted in "The Shining Note," in John Updike, *Hugging the Shore* (New York: Vintage Books, 1984), p. 195.

20. *Lake County News,* Lake County, California. Authors have a xerox copy of this updated article.

21. John Updike, "On One's Own Oeuvre," in *Hugging the Shore* (New York: Vintage Books, 1984), p. 868.

22. "A Separate Realty," in *Rocky Mountain Magazine,* January-February 1981.

23. American Law Institute, *A Model Land Development Code,* complete text, adopted by the American Law Institute May 21, 1975, with Reporter's Commentary (Philadelphia: American Law Institute, 1976), pp. ix-x.

24. Henry James, *The American Scene* (New York: Washington Square Books, 1983), p. xxii.

CHAPTER

3

Capturing the Benefits of Growth

As long as people have lived together in towns, they have expected their leaders to provide the necessities for community life. In the Dark Ages, this meant castles and walls; later, it meant public quays to service textile trade and canals to turn waterwheels. Later still, when the causes of lethal epidemics such as cholera were discovered and widely known, clean water supplies and reliable sewage disposal became a necessity. Today in the United States, citizens have come to expect municipal governments to provide a wide range of expensive and sophisticated public necessities, paid for principally from tax levies on property. Modern towns are in the business of furnishing services to citizens, who are also voters and who judge the quality of their leaders by the cost and quality of the services delivered.

Leaders indeed enjoy certain options with which they can satisfy their constituents. Provided that tax revenues grow, they can either reduce levies or increase services. And since until recently municipalities found that the property taxes paid by new residents more than offset the additional costs of providing common services for them, it has been an article of faith that growth would mean greater tax revenues for a more pleasing community life.

FISCAL IMPACT METHODS

In the late 1960s and early 1970s, appraising growth solely in terms of tax revenues came into question. High inflation rates increased munici-pal costs and frustrated many towns' attempts to provide traditional public services for citizens new and old. The relationship between growth and local finance became, for once, not always positive, and municipalities began analyzing proposed development in terms of its effects on city budgets; for example, how much additional revenue a new subdivision would bring was compared to how much additional public spending it would require. A typical assumption of such a comparison (known commonly as *fiscal impact analysis*) would be that because most changes in local government's services and taxes reflect changes in population, the costs and revenues of such changes can therefore be estimated. For example, by predicting how many additional school children are likely to reside in a newly built subdivision, the fiscal analyst can estimate how many new teachers and school buildings will be necessary.

Early proponents of fiscal impact analysis believed their work would be "of considerable importance to local decisionmaking and planning"[1] because it would increase understanding of the fiscal consequences of growth. In many states during the 1970s, such scrutiny of probable revenues and costs became a routine part of the review process for proposed developments. Gradually, however, some limitations of fiscal impact analysis became clear to laymen and even better known to courts.[2] Particularly limiting was the use of this analysis in arguments against unpopular low-income projects in the name of fiscal prudence, and its inability to take into account nonfiscal benefits provided by development. Consequently, revised editions of fiscal impact manuals introduced warnings that fiscal impacts were only one of several effects of growth, and reminded fiscal impact enthusiasts that local governments were, in fact, something more than businesses: they were guardians of a public interest more broadly defined than municipal budgets.

More recently, in places where rapid population growth required new infrastructure such as schools, roadways, and water and sewerage lines, leaders found their budgets simply could not do it all. Fiscal impact methods, by demonstrating the connection between new growth and increased municipal costs, helped suggest that a logical source of money for public works might be the very developers whose projects were creating the need for new public facilities. The idea, then, of providing infrastructure or payments in lieu of infrastructure gradually became accepted as a cost of doing business in many rapidly growing areas.[3] Today, hundreds of towns use fiscal impact analysis to determine the costs of development;[4] moreover, they expect developers to underwrite directly many of the costs specifically attributable to facilities their development projects require.[5] This new fiscal impact analysis must use constitutional methods for apportioning costs of public improvements. It must also be judged equitable with regard to who is paying the charge, how much they will pay, and whether the full cost of a service is paid by those who use it.[6] Courts in several states have tested local impact fee ordinances on these very grounds.

Some jurisdictions, equally convinced of the connection between growth and public costs, have sought to avoid the constitutional problems of apportioning costs among new and old residents. One simple alternative draws special district boundaries around areas of recent growth and makes the people living there solely responsible for the public facilities they need. Census Bureau statistics demonstrate that this is a popular way to make newcomers pay for their own capital needs. During the 20 years prior to 1982, the number of municipalities in the United States grew by only 6 percent, while the number of special districts rose 57 percent (from 18,323 to almost 29,000), an increase which, importantly, does not include school districts.[7] But these special financing districts have created another problem that only now is becoming clear. The special districts provide so many ordinary governmental services that general governments have lost some of their traditional authority to guide and control growth, and even to govern in a comprehensive manner.[8]

Public administration journals regularly review the shortcomings of fiscal impact methods. Typically, writers chronicle the progress of court cases or else seek to prove that fiscal impact analysis is inadequate because it ignores the nonmonetary issues involved in development. Despite this, fiscal impact analysis in one or another of its evolutionary forms is still the most popular tool for evaluating the dynamics of public finance in quickly growing areas. Its premises are easy to grasp and its methods relatively simple. Moreover, fiscal impact analysis has been especially agreeable because it can be and has been used to require newcomers to help "pay their own way."

But What if Growth Isn't Rapid?

Continuing professional interest in fiscal impact analysis has principally focused on the problems of rapidly growing areas. Yet municipal fiscal problems also exist where growth is not rapid. This book proposes an evolution of fiscal impact analysis which takes into account the fact that even slow growth can be a problem if it is not carefully managed.

Some descriptive information from the state of Montana is offered here as background. The small population of this large state is widely dispersed, and the cost of delivering ordinary public services even around the few urbanized areas is high. Local governments cannot, however, easily reduce per capita costs because growth occurs at too modest a rate. Indeed, several cities have been overly optimistic in approving subdivisions and making loans for public improvements in them, and taxpayers have had to repay loans for useless facilities when lots have failed to sell and developers have defaulted.[9]

The inadequacy of municipal budgets is evident in the lamentable state of public infrastructure. In Montana, as in many other states, voters have rejected bond issues and passed limitations on state and local taxing authority. Unwilling to impose higher taxes, yet constitutionally required to balance their budgets, many local governments have saved money by neglecting ordinary maintenance of public facilities. While the effects of this neglect may have been invisible early on, severe deterioration of public assets has finally appeared, as well as a large gap between capital needs and the money to pay for them. In Gallatin County, for example, there is a state-built bridge worth $410,000 which cannot be used because the county has no funds to repair the roads that lead to it. Indeed, 75 percent of the streets in Montana—those solely the responsibility of city governments—need major repair or reconstruction.[10]

In most instances capital facilities cannot be added incrementally, but must be erected in advance to a predetermined size that is in excess of demand. Consequently, many local jurisdictions carry a substantial investment in oversized infrastructure. In part, this is the familiar result of a tradition in public finance that one generation will help pay for another generation's infrastructure.[11] But there can be little doubt that unguided growth has also contributed to oversized infrastructure. Consider briefly the case of new development locating within a service district holding excess capacity. Here, as the numbers of residents increase, the same obligated payment for preexisting infrastructure can be spread across a greater tax base, and mill levies can fall over the useful life of the capital facilities. Moreover, as will be shown later, the operating efficiency of infrastructure can be improved with increasing numbers of users. However, if new development goes outside the reach of existing facilities, new residents do not use the excess capacity built precisely in anticipation of the population growth they represent, nor do they pay for it. For this reason, a scattered and expansive growth pattern may cause prior investment to be underutilized and excess capacity to go to waste; it may also mean the tax base is inadequate to pay off past investments and to maintain infrastructure already in place. In such circumstances, the notion of older generations providing for future generations becomes no more than a foolish investment. The problem, of course, is particularly intractable where growth is slow, since the opportunities to influence location decisions arise less frequently than where population increases quickly.

There is a familiar argument which says that if a developer chooses to "privatize" the cost of infrastructure—for example, by building a small sewage treatment facility, or by installing a common septic system in a new subdivision—the public cost is zero. This line of reasoning is, however, erroneous. When new residents settle outside the reach of existing facilities, they neither pay taxes to reduce the per capita debt burdens underwriting those facilities, nor do they increase the demand for service and in so doing increase the efficiency of the older plant's operation. For both these reasons, there is a public cost of "privatizing," one that some scholars suggest cities should charge to new development for the obvious reason that "it created the need for it in the first place."[12]

Many states show signs of suffering from these hidden costs. Dispersed development patterns have meant that local governments frequently pay very high costs for connecting users to capital facilities such as public water supplies, for making such services as fire protection available to scattered users, and for bringing users to a capital facility such as a school building. At the same time, growth in one location which leaves unused capacity in another costs the state dearly because of undermaintained and excessively underutilized infrastructure.[13]

COMMITTED LANDS ANALYSIS

Committed lands analysis is suggested as a branch of fiscal impact research to be used where expansive development has resulted in excessive capital projects whose costs cannot quickly be reduced. Committed lands analysis would be appropriate, for example, in jurisdictions such as in Montana, where school buses drive long miles to pick up just a few children, or where sewerage lines run past undeveloped lands to reach even more distant subdivisions. Because in a practical sense local governments have committed themselves to providing services there, the phrase *committed lands* describes the vacant tracts that lie within governmental service districts. If growth could be directed to these committed lands, rather than allowed to spread where new infrastructure would have to be extended, public costs of development would undoubtedly be reduced.[14]

Reducing public costs by guiding growth might seem an obviously agreeable concept. However, many American citizens have high regard for individual property rights, an attitude which promotes skepticism about governmental interference with private enterprise. For this reason, growth has been guided primarily by private decisions to subdivide and sell land, and these decisions are made without serious regard to efficient use of public capital facilities. However, in places where public infrastructure is deteriorated, and where modest rates of growth are probable, citizens must answer two previously ignored questions:

Under what conditions do municipalities, as they create infrastructure, incur an obligation to guide the location of growth so as to utilize and pay for that infrastructure?

Under what conditions do municipalities incur a responsibility to guide the location of growth so as to minimize the costs of public service delivery?

In formulating their response, most citizens would concede that taxpayers, in approving bond issues to build capital facilities, expect their local government to operate those facilities at the lowest possible cost and to guard the public investment represented. Under certain identifiable circumstances, such expectations could come to mean guiding the very location of growth.

Such circumstances arguably exist wherever public infrastructure is badly deteriorated, where the cost of delivering services is high, and where there is popular opposition to raising property taxes. Also, if local communities are to continue to exist as places where residents find personal satisfaction and where new enterprises want to locate, it is imperative to use public assets efficiently. As a labor leader put it:

We need to recognize that to promote a good business climate you need excellent public services, a sound infrastructure, strong educational institutions and an economy that seeks to improve the quality of life for its workers.[15]

Committed lands analysis argues that future growth should be located so as to increase the efficiency of existing municipal public works. Two simple questions express the practical test of a government's efficiency: "What does it provide for the people, and what does it cost the people?"[16] Committed lands analysis uses an economist's formulation to set the same questions: efficiency means producing and distributing services that people want without wasting resources. This definition of efficiency contains two components:

1. Efficient production of services from major public assets; and
2. Efficient distribution of services.

The narrative sections that follow will develop the economic issues implicit in this two-part definition of efficiency, and will show how this definition can be used to identify locations where growth would promote greater municipal efficiency. The discussion in this essay provides the rationale for the methods of calculation that appear in Chapter 4.

In formulating the following sections, the authors have been guided by the premise that the analysis must be theoretically rigorous, yet its methods must be simple, easy to comprehend, and inexpensive to implement if they are to become a routine part of decisionmaking. To meet these goals, the expository material about efficiency uses the formal laws of production economics, while the methods of calculation use certain of the more commonly understood methods of fiscal impact analysis.

Efficiency Component 1: Production of Services from Major Public Assets

The economic issues of using public assets in an efficient fashion can be discussed by applying the concepts of production economics to a typical public capital asset such as a wastewater treatment plant. The discussion will assume the plant can handle a greater capacity than was needed at the time of its construction, an assumption in keeping with most cities' reliance on continued population growth.

As applied to private firms, a production function is the "technical relationship telling the maximum amount of output capable of being produced by each and every set of specified inputs . . . for a given state of technical knowledge."[17] In the case of public facilities, *output* can be understood as the level of service demanded by the public. Using the example of a wastewater treatment plant, output is the number of gallons that must be processed. With this adaptation, the production function for a public asset takes the form shown in Figure 1, Graph A. This graph depicts the relationship between gallons processed and two standard input factors, capital and labor. The *input factor ratio* of employees/capital is used to signify mathematically that output, i.e., demand for a level of service, can be met either by increasing the number of employees for a given utilization of a capital facility, or by using the facility more efficiently without changing the number of employees.

The proper reading of Graph A shows that greater volumes of wastewater can be treated by increasing the use of the facility and adding laborers, up to the point labeled as maximum output. Beyond this point, demand is so high that output falls as a consequence of too much labor. If, for example, additional workers were hired to force 11 million gallons through a water treatment plant designed to process only 9 million, their attempts could cause the system to clog, rupture, or let through untreated water. In any case, only 7 million gallons of wastewater may be adequately processed.

Economists have derived the formal features of production theory from Graph A and shown them to be both mathematically sound and empirically reliable.[18] By calculating the first derivative of the output line shown on Graph A with respect to each of the input factors, Graphs B and C can be drawn. The first derivatives are the marginal products of each factor, i.e., the change in output that occurs either as employees increase and capital is held constant, or as capital increases and the number of employees is constant. Graph B shows the marginal product for employees, and Graph C represents the marginal product for capital.[19]

The mathematical qualities of the marginal product curves shown in these two graphs allow economists to classify three stages of production:

Stage I. One variable input (either capital or labor, in the example used here) has a positive marginal product, while the other is negative;

Stage II. Both variable inputs have positive marginal products; and

Stage III. One variable input (either labor or capital) will have a positive marginal product, while the other is negative. The positive input in Stage I will be negative in Stage III; and the negative input in Stage I will be positive in Stage III.

Graph B shows that in Stage II the marginal product of employees is positive, indicating that total output is rising. However, in Stage III the marginal product of employees is negative, meaning t' at total output decreases. Similarly, Graph C shows the marginal products for capital.

FIGURE 1. Production Function for a Wastewater Treatment Plant

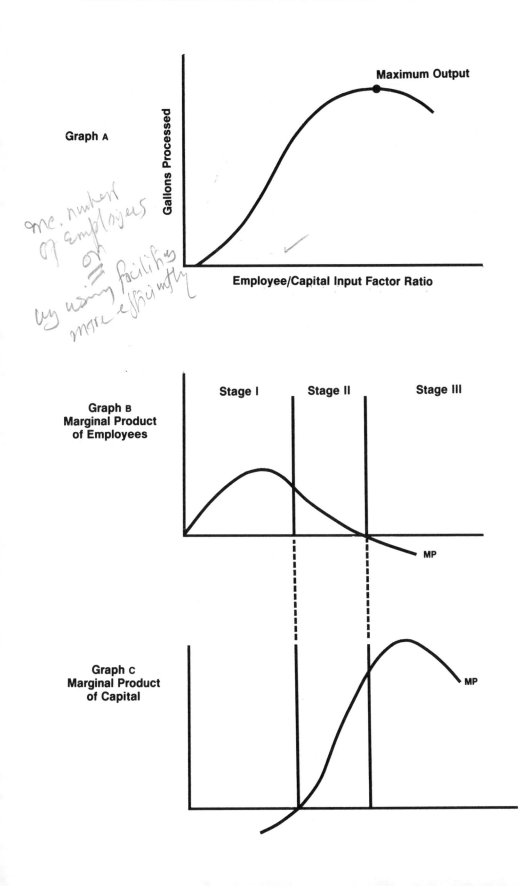

Graph A

Gallons Processed

Maximum Output

Employee/Capital Input Factor Ratio

Graph B
Marginal Product
of Employees

Stage I   Stage II   Stage III

MP

Graph C
Marginal Product
of Capital

MP

inc. number
of employees
on
by using facilities
more efficiently

On a portion of this graph, the marginal product is negative, indicating that output has been reduced as a consequence of too much capital, low demand, and a given number of employees. For example, using a wastewater treatment plant capable of processing 9 million gallons to clean only 1 million undoubtedly means excessive maintenance for pumps, holding tanks, and aeration facilities that are barely used. In Stage II, however, the marginal product of additional capital is positive. Taken together, Graphs B and C show that only in Stage II are both capital and labor capable of being used efficiently. For this reason, Stage II is known as the rational range of production.

Figure 2 illustrates more dynamically the problems of efficiency in providing public services. Graph D simply repeats the production function of the wastewater treatment facility, with the addition of two lines. The first, a line drawn horizontally from the point *OZ*, represents the maximum technical capacity of the treatment plant; the second, line *AA'*, represents some single arbitrary number of gallons to be treated. Graph E is the constant product curve drawn from Graph D[20] and represents all combinations of capital and employees that can treat the quantity *AA'* gallons of wastewater in all three stages of production. This graph can be understood by continuing the example offered earlier.

Assume that the maximum technical capacity of the wastewater treatment plant is 9 million gallons, and that existing residents and businesses produce 6 million gallons of wastewater. This existing demand is represented on Graph E by line *AA'*. Graph E shows all the operating options the plant's manager has for cleaning 6 million gallons of wastewater (demand level *AA'*). If the plant were fully utilized (represented by *OZ* in Graph E), the manager would have to employ *OY* workers in order to meet demand. But this choice uses resources inefficiently, a fact formally explained by production economists as capital operating in Stage III while labor operates in Stage I. Put in simple terms, such a choice is inefficient because other combinations of capital and labor could process *AA'* gallons of wastewater by using fewer resources. For example, *AA'* gallons of wastewater could be treated by using *OW* capital and employing *OR* workers. (However, if the manager were to employ only *OR* people to operate the plant at *OZ* capacity, the result as shown in Graph E would be that something less than *AA'* gallons of wastewater would be treated.) The choice to operate the facility at its full capacity is inefficient when the quantity of wastewater to be treated is less than that full capacity.

FIGURE 2.

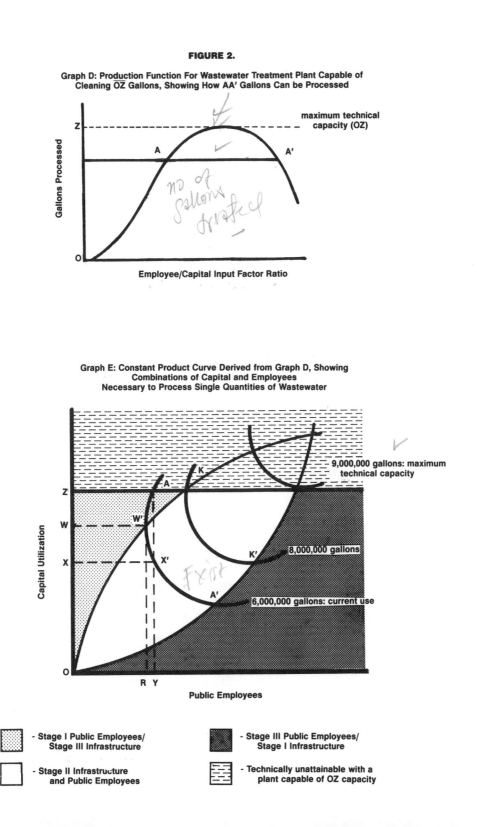

Graph D: Production Function For Wastewater Treatment Plant Capable of Cleaning O̅Z̅ Gallons, Showing How AA' Gallons Can be Processed

Graph E: Constant Product Curve Derived from Graph D, Showing Combinations of Capital and Employees Necessary to Process Single Quantities of Wastewater

But even the choice of *OW* capital and *OR* workers is inefficient. Operating the wastewater treatment plant at level *OW* means that *WZ* of the plant is not being used. Despite the fact that only *OR* employees are necessary to process *AA'* gallons of wastewater and that production efficiency is improved because part of the facility is idle, neither fixed costs associated with *WZ* capital nor maintenance costs related to weather, aging, and material deterioration will decrease. Such costs are not related to output, although existing users pay for them. This means that the choice to operate only part of the facility results in excessive fixed costs for existing users. The excessive costs are caused by inadequate demand for service from a plant capable of *OZ* utilization.

Graph E shows that other combinations of labor and capital will process *AA'* gallons of wastewater. In no case, however, can the plant manager avoid *underutilizing* capital to a considerable extent. Only as the total number of gallons to be processed moves from line *AA'* toward full capacity can the plant be used more efficiently. For example, line *KK'* on Graph E represents the demand that 8 million gallons be treated. On this line, fixed capital is used more efficiently than at any point on line *AA'*.

For all these reasons, line *AA'* on Graph E illustrates the problem of too little demand, an oversized capital asset, and inescapable inefficiency in the provision of public services. It also shows that obstacles to efficiency come primarily from inadequate demand, not from a failure to use employees or capital in a least-cost combination.[21] In the private sector, inadequate demand can be met either by undertaking marketing strategies to increase demand, or by shutting down the operation and investing in more profitable activities. This cannot be the case when government provides such essential services for community life as sewage treatment, clean water, minimum level of education, and so forth. Governments cannot use marketing to stimulate demand substantially, they cannot reduce prices to increase demand,[22] and they cannot responsibly shut down services when faced with inefficiency.

The manager of the wastewater treatment plant faces an intractable dilemma as long as demand does not go above level *AA'*. To use less than all of the existing capacity is to burden existing users with excessive costs. To use full capacity is to pay for more workers than necessary. And since marketing strategies for governmental services are ineffectual, the manager cannot cause existing users to demand more service. In fact, the rational range of production can only be reached with more users, whose increased demand for wastewater treatment will allow the plant to be operated more efficiently.[23]

This discussion can be readily applied to the important issue of where growth is to take place. If new households locate outside the service area of the water treatment facility, service demand will go no higher than level *AA'*, causing all the inefficient production results described above. But both the manager's inability to use the facility efficiently and the existing users' excessive payments for fixed costs could be remedied if new residents were within the geographic service area of the public water treatment system. Their additional demand for service could allow more efficient use of the water treatment plant, and their additional taxes would reduce the per capita fixed costs of the plant. In fact, assuring demand by directing growth may well be the only way to manage public assets efficiently in slow growing areas.

Although different public assets have different production functions, the meaning and the definitions of the stages of production are invariant. In all cases, Stage II, the rational range of production, is desirable. Where Stage II begins and ends is an empirical question requiring sophisticated analysis of individual capital facilities, an undertaking beyond the capability of most jurisdictions for whom committed lands analysis is intended. For this reason, we suggest common-sense indicators that additional demand would bring greater efficiency to the operations of large public assets. The first such indicator would be growth projections showing that full utilization of a town's public facilities would not be reached within the productive life of those facilities. A second would be outsized public facilities going unused by newly constructed commercial establishments or subdivisions. A third would be extensions or additions to the menu of public services a town provides, despite evidence that existing infrastructure is inadequately maintained. If any of these conditions exist, a town could benefit from guiding development so as to increase the use and efficiency of existing public facilities.

The conditions described above are typical of the short-run operating conditions of public facilities. Economists define the short run as a period within which the physical plant or capital stock cannot be changed. As Chapter 4 will explain, committed lands analysis uses the costs of a public asset for a budgetary year as the basis for evaluating efficiency. Using the budgetary year as the definition of short run requires some clarification because it is not commonly used in the economic analysis familiar to planners—analysis most typically based on the private sector. Economists now know, however, that the measurement of costs in the private sector is different from the public sector. Economists divide short run private sector costs into two categories: variable costs and fixed costs. In studying the economics of large public facilities, these two categories stand, although the particular items included in each have been changed. The reason for this change in classification follows from the fact that large public assets provide essential services in such a way that inputs do not vary with the level of output to any great extent. That is, a significant number of cost items that are variable in the private sector are fixed in the public sector. This distinction between the two sectors is fundamental to the methods of committed lands analysis.

To make the distinction between costs in the public and private sectors more clear, economic research has developed a menu of costs illustrative of each sector. As explained earlier in this chapter, managers of private firms can vary inputs over a wide range because they have several options. If a firm faces a shortage of demand, its management can reduce the supply of labor, buy fewer raw materials, and even shut down production where it is not profitable; firms can also advertise, lower prices, and create new products to stimulate demand. Managers of essential public services simply do not have these options. They cannot lay off workers, reduce the purchase of raw materials, or shut down unprofitable operations; neither can they advertise, lower prices, or promote new services.

Economists now recognize that essential differences in operations mean that many variable costs in the private sector are fixed costs to managers of public facilities. Large public facilities are operated by a small number of workers who can provide a relatively wide range of output. For this reason, economists consider labor costs to be fixed. Economists also treat many operating costs of public facilities as fixed, because the facilities are typically designed and operated so that raw materials are a known proportion of output per year, and the output is treated as if it were known for the budgetary period (though it may vary from one day to the next). These costs would be variable to private sector firms.[24]

Because economists consider public facilities to be fixed-cost production units, they know that average fixed costs will decline over any range of output below full capacity. They also know that any average variable costs of providing public services can be considered constant over the range of output, and can be understood to be small. As an example, consider the costs of putting out a house fire. The fixed costs are large because they must include having the firefighting apparatus and manpower available. The variable cost—the price of gasoline to drive to the fire—is small, and a constant cost per mile driven. The fact that variable costs are small relative to fixed costs means that the efficiency of public assets is properly concerned with fixed costs. Committed lands analysis has used this economic understanding of how public facilities are managed to define the way that efficiency can be measured.

A final comment is in order for the reader trained in private sector measures of efficiency who expects marginal cost criteria to inform management decisions. It was remarked above that average variable costs are constant over the range of output. Remembering that marginal cost is the change in total cost for each change in output, a constant average variable cost means that marginal and average costs are equal.[25]

Chapter 4 will discuss methods to measure the changes in production efficiency. Yet, production is only one part of the definition of efficiency used by committed lands analysis. The following discussion will consider the other part of that definition, the distribution of services.

Efficiency Component II: Distribution of Services

Efficiency, once again, can be said to mean: *distribution of what the public wants without wasting resources.* And "what the public wants" can be interpreted to mean the level of service that the public expects. Fiscal impact analysis directs its users to assume that current local service levels reliably indicate the standards to which a community is accustomed, and, moreover, the standards which they expect to be maintained in the foreseeable future.[26] Existing conditions of roadways, the response capability of the fire department, and the frequency of street-cleaning, accordingly, are all thought to be the surest indications of what the public expects. Taxpayers might *want* better service, but they are apparently unwilling to pay for it. Committed lands analysis will use this assumption, and will calculate as costs to new users only those expenditures necessary to maintain the existing level of service delivery.

The second part of the efficiency definition, "without wasting resources," has to do with the subject of the actual cost of delivering services to users. Committed lands analysis focuses on the costs of delivery that are directly related to the location of users, and assumes that costs related to method of delivery do not change according to location. For example, a new engineering study may suggest methods to make pothole repairs last longer; however, such a suggestion could improve maintenance of roadways regardless of the location of new residents. It is in this way that all matters concerning method of delivery can be held neutral.

It should be noted that the phrase "delivery of services" is a general term meant to refer to all the ways services are actually provided to users. In some instances, users come to the physical plant to receive services (as is the case with public education); in others, services extend to users (as is the case with water and sewerage systems); in still others, services are taken to the users on demand (as is the case with fire protection). But in every case, committed lands analysis will estimate the costs of distributing services as those costs which are related to location of users. At its simplest, this will entail determining the cost per unit of distance, multiplied by the added distance to a new user. How these estimations will be made is the subject of Chapter 4.

With respect to location-related costs, contemporary research suggests that services can be distributed to new users without wasting resources in one of two ways. Resources will not be wasted if there is no additional delivery cost associated with a new user. If, for example, a new subdivision is located within walking distance of a public school, taxpayers will bear no additional cost of busing. Likewise, if a commercial establishment is built on land already serviced by a sewerage main, there is no additional public cost of connecting the new establishment to the wastewater treatment plant. In cases such as these, the addition of new users will cause increased demand for public services and allow gains in production efficiency. However, if a new user is located where services are not already provided, there will be new costs associated with delivery. These costs would be subtracted from the gains in production efficiency, and only if the result were positive would the analyst conclude a net gain in efficient use of public assets was possible.

Committed Lands Appear

This discussion of efficiency gives rise to an economist's description of *committed lands:* places where increased production efficiency can be achieved through additional demand, and where the additional cost of delivery is no greater than the value of that increased production efficiency. Chapter 4 will describe how to calculate these values and costs. Once those calculations are made, a map could be drawn delineating boundaries of areas where the cost of service delivery is less than the value of gains in production efficiency. Consider a hypothetical example. Assume it had been calculated that each new user of a wastewater treatment plant would bring $1,500 in increased production efficiency, and that the cost of collecting sewage was $5 per linear foot. Simple division would show that as long as new users were within 300 feet of the existing sewerage network, increased operational efficiency would result from allowing those new users to connect to the wastewater treatment system. The committed lands analyst could use this information to draw a 300-foot perimeter around the existing network of sewage treatment lines. The area within the perimeter would be committed lands for the sewage treatment plant.

This process of drawing perimeters would be repeated for each public asset within a jurisdiction, resulting in a vivid illustration of the concept of committed lands. If these invested lands were shaded, the maps would show areas where new development would result in a net increase in efficiency for each public asset. Because of the characteristics of production in the services themselves, it can be safely assumed that output of each does not affect costs in the others at the margin.[27] This characteristic allows the shaded perimeter maps for each public asset to be overlaid.

Figure 3 roughly depicts the result. Using only three services (for the sake of visual clarity), Figure 3 identifies service areas for sewage treatment, fire protection, and water supply. These are areas where excess capacity exists, and where the cost of distribution is less than the gain in production efficiency for each service. Overlaying the maps of these areas illustrates that in Area A all services are provided; in Area B fire and sewer are available, and in Area C only fire protection. Development located in Area A would offer the greatest gains in community-wide efficiency. A decision to locate in Area C would require new investment in sewer and water services, despite the community's having already invested in such infrastructure in Area A. The result of such a decision would be no gains in efficiency from increased use, and no reduction in the fixed costs of existing sewer and water facilities.

The point to the map is simple: it highlights committed lands. It also suggests where capital improvements should occur next, in as much as it will always be better to extend any single service into areas that have the greatest number of other facilities with excess capacity. The map would be useful to public officials because it gives them reliable information about where development should be encouraged and where capital facilities should be extended as population grows.[28]

CONCLUSION

The aim of committed lands analysis is to show how new development can be used to achieve greater efficiency in public services in those places where growth is relatively slow. The analysis takes existing characteristics of public capital facilities—where the plants are, their capacity, how services are provided—and attempts to improve their efficiency by directing the location of growth. The concern here is not to find the reason that existing infrastructure is underutilized. That is plain enough: plants that are too large could result from enthusiasm for a new technology, overeager competition for federal subsidies, inaccurate population projections, or laissez-faire development decisions. Finding the reasons for our public mistakes is no trivial matter, but it is simply outside the interest of this book. The interests here are simply these: public investments exist, they cannot easily be reduced, and so prudent public policy would have them used as efficiently as possible. In an

Figure 3. Committed Lands Map

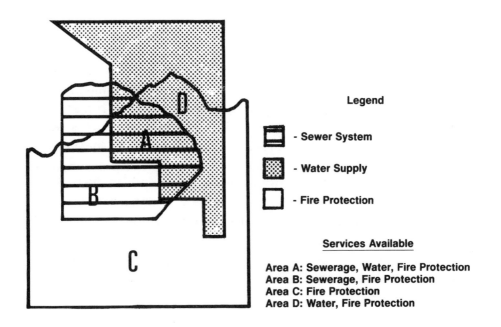

Legend

☐ - Sewer System

▦ - Water Supply

☐ - Fire Protection

Services Available

Area A: Sewerage, Water, Fire Protection
Area B: Sewerage, Fire Protection
Area C: Fire Protection
Area D: Water, Fire Protection

important sense, committed lands analysis can serve as a transitional method; it provides guidance to a community trying to move from inefficient to efficient use of each existing capital asset. While transitional decision-making cannot quickly alter the results of a municipality's oversized and undermaintained infrastructure, it can practically and prudently begin to manage growth; it can make past capital investments more efficient; and it can guide decisions about such investments in the future.

Thus far, committed lands analysis has been described from the point of view of the taxpayer. However, the analysis will be useful to developers as well. By using the methods described here and by making the simple calculations that will be explained in Chapter 4, developers can identify sites most likely to promote public efficiency. For example, in public hearings developers could cite clearer advantages to having their projects approved, and development within committed lands could be backed by a public interest in efficiency. Moreover, the developer, by increasing the likelihood of approval, would enjoy higher expected returns. Because of the clear public gains to be gotten from guiding growth, Chapter 5 will discuss appropriate incentives for encouraging developers to choose sites in committed lands.

While committed lands analysis was conceived for Montana, its suitability for any jurisdiction in similar circumstances should be clear. The number of such jurisdictions is not small. In fact, over 20 percent of the counties in the United States have characteristics similar to those that gave rise to this book,[29] and the costs of inefficient use of the public assets in those counties has to be significant.

Where growth forecasts are gloomy or modest, leaders cannot take a reactive position with regard to public investments: government needs to make them pay off. That means using such growth as comes to the benefit of residents who previously invested in commodious public facilities. As a tool of public policy, management of demand is a neglected subject.[30] Committed lands analysis seeks to end the neglect of this important issue. Just as early fiscal impact analysis highlighted the connection between growth and public costs, and suggested the reasonableness of expecting growth to help pay for itself, so the concept of committed lands highlights the relationship between location of growth and public costs, and suggests the importance of guiding development so as to manage demand.

NOTES

1. Management Technology Exchange Program, *Fiscal Impact: Subdivision and Annexation Review*, p. 2. This publication is available from the Montana State Department of Commerce, Cogswell Building, Helena, Montana.

2. For a thorough review of the early cases involving appropriate application of fiscal impact analysis, see Robert W. Burchell and David Listokin, Appendix I: "National Summary of Case Law Relating to Cost-Revenue," in *The Fiscal Impact Handbook* (New Brunswick, New Jersey: Center for Urban Policy Research, 1978), pp. 328–350.

3. Douglas R. Porter, "Will Developers Pay to Play?" *Journal of the American Planning Association* 54 (Winter 1988): 72–75.

4. James E. Frank and Paul B. Downing, "Patterns of Impact Fee Usage," Paper presented at the American Planning Association National Conference, April 1987.

5. Douglas R. Porter, "The Rights and Wrongs of Impact Fees," *Urban Land* (July 1986): 16.

6. See for example Michael A. Stegman, "Development Fees for Infrastructure," *Urban Land* (May 1986): 2–3; and Timothy Beatley, "Ethical Issues in the Use of Impact Fees to Finance Community Growth," paper presented to the American Planning Association National Conference, April 1987.

7. John Hebers, "Take Me Home, Country Roads," *Planning* 53 (November 1987): 7.

8. Ibid., p. 7.

9. Montana law allows a local government to create a special improvement district, known colloquially as an SID, and sell tax-exempt, low-interest bonds to finance improvements such as streets and water lines within a district drawn to encompass a new subdivision. The proceeds of the bonds are loaned to developers on the understanding they will be paid off as the subdivision lots sell. However, should the developer fail, the responsibility for repaying bond investors falls on local government, which must levy taxes for such repayment. In Missoula, for example, delinquent SIDs on 11 projects amounted to $1.19 million; interest payments on these bonds are about $300,000 per year. And in Bozeman it is estimated that taxpayers will be assessed $5.8 million over the next 15 years for delinquent SID payments for a single failed subdivision. (*Missoulian*, October 8, 1986).

10. Governor's Task Force on Infrastructure, *Final Report* (Helena, Montana: December 1984), pp. 30–31.

11. Thomas P. Snyder and Michael A. Stegman, *Paying for Growth* (Washington, D.C.: Urban Land Institute, 1987), p. 19.

12. *Ibid*, p. 29.

13. In some areas of the state, certain natural factors (specifically, the lack of water) have prevented a spread-out growth pattern. If a proposed subdivision requires city or county-provided water, its developer must be responsive to local government's concerns, which certainly include an analysis of how far the jurisdiction can afford to run its water supply lines. But where water is both abundant and relatively easy to get, local officials are left in the position of responding to what has been decided outside their powers.

14. Bruce Weber and Richard Beck, writing in the series *Coping with Growth* aver that "Almost every study on the subject concludes that sprawl—noncontiguous, low-density development—results in higher public costs than compact development . . ." See "Minimizing Public Costs of Residential Growth," (Oregon State University: Western Rural Development Center, March 1979.)

15. *Missoulian*, July 18, 1987.

16. James Bryce, Viscount, *The American Commonwealth* (New York: Macmillan Company, 1918), p. 147.

17. Paul A. Samuelson, *Economics*,

10th Ed. (New York: McGraw-Hill, 1976), p. 537.

18. See Edwin Mansfield, ed., *Microeconomics: Theory and Applications*, 3rd ed. (New York: Norton, 1979), pp. 200–210.

19. The calculation of the partial derivative with respect to capital results in Graph C, most easily interpreted as being read left to right, while Graph B is read right to left. This is inherent in the mathematics involved.

20. This constant product curve, known as an isoquant graph, is derivable from Graph D using standard tools of production economics. See, for example, C. E. Ferguson, *Microeconomic Theory* (Homewood, Illinois: Irwin, 1966), pp. 131–150.

21. For a mathematical proof and exposition of these properties of the production efficiency question addressed here, see J. M. Henderson and R. E. Quandt, *Microeconomic Theory: A Mathematical Approach* (New York City: McGraw-Hill, 1971), pp. 58–60.

22. Most public services are insensitive to price, as is the case with sewage treatment: lowering the cost to clean water will probably not result in a household's creating more waste. Other services are priced according to statutory directives that charges collect no more than necessary to cover costs, in which case a price reduction would mean the service would be provided for less than it costs.

23. Economists will note that this solution will improve capital utilization at all price ratios of capital to employees within the rational range of production for output levels above *AA'*.

24. The reason many public services are not privately provided is that a single plant most efficiently produces them, a condition economists refer to as a natural monopoly.

25. Several citations will guide the interested reader. The mathematical derivation appears in J. Henderson and R. Quandt, *Microeconomic Theory* (New York:

McGraw-Hill, 1948), p. 48. A description of the behavioral aspects of the production process in the private sector, with applications for the public sector appears in A. S. Eichmer, *Toward a New Economics* (New York: M.E. Sharpe, 1985), pp. 35–43. A discussion of the labor market and the case of labor being a fixed factor in production appears in I. Rima, *Labor Markets, Wages and Employment* (New York: Norton, 1981), pp. 136–140. And finally several articles provide the empirical cost analysis underlying fixed factor proportions. Among them are: Alan A. Walters, "Production and Cost, An Econometric Survey," *Econometrica* 31: 1–66; Bella Gold, "New Perspectives on Cost Theory and Empirical Findings," *Journal of Industrial Economics* 14: 164–89; L. S. Zudak, "Labor Demand and Multiproduct Cost in Semicontinuous and Multiprocessed Facilities," *Journal of Industrial Economics* 19: 267–90.

26. A typical statement of these assumptions is "current local service levels are the most accurate indicators of future service levels and . . . they will continue on the same scale in the future." R. Burchell, D. Listokin, and W. Dolphin, *The New Practitioner's Guide to Fiscal Impact Analysis* (New Brunswick, New Jersey: Center for Urban Policy Research, 1985), p. 14.

27. Consider the case of firefighting, which will use some quantity of the water supply. However, fires are fought only sporadically and the actual usage of water will be negligible.

28. It is important to note that leapfrogged development may, in fact, be the most efficient in order to take advantage of preexisting capacity in expensive public facilities.

29. We totaled the population living in urbanized portions of counties where the persons per square mile was no greater than Missoula County's (this being the proxy measure for dispersed population), and which had grown more slowly between 1970 and 1980 than the national average (this being the proxy measure for modest growth). Source: U.S. Bureau of the Census, *1980 Census of Populations; Characteristics of the Population,* Volume I, Part I: "U.S. Summary: Land Area, Population and Population Density."

30. Capital facilities planning is con

cerned with the orderly extension of public assets. But this branch of municipal management generally assumes that investment in capital facilities will attract growth and as a theory does not promote aggressive policies to see that actually they do.

4

Committed Lands Analysis

This chapter will explain how the underlying concepts of committed lands analysis can be transformed into formulas for measuring how the location of new customers affects the efficiency of large public capital facilities. New customers include inhabitants of newly built houses, as well as new commercial and industrial establishments—all land uses implicit in the notion of growth.

Committed lands analysis can serve three broad purposes. First, it should allow a community to determine which of its existing public facilities have excess capacity, and for those that do, to estimate the value of the gains in efficiency that each additional customer would bring. This information would indicate the service districts in which new development would bring fiscal benefits to the community. Such a determination could be the basis of a policy which takes public capital facilities— where the plants are and what their capacity is; where customers are and how services are provided to them—and attempts to improve their efficiency by directing the location of growth. To keep up with land use decisions and budgetary changes in its jurisdiction, a local government would make this determination once a year.

The second purpose of committed lands analysis is to define unambiguously the public benefits of a private decision to develop land. By using the methods to be described here, a developer could identify sites most likely to promote public efficiency and could estimate the value of that increased efficiency. Subsequently, in public hearings developers could cite clear advantages to having their projects approved, and development in committed lands could be backed by a public interest in efficiency.

Finally, committed lands analysis could allow an orderly assessment of long term capital needs, and even help make long term location decisions. While the approach is incremental, making increasingly better use of existing capital facilities with the construction of each new building, the accumulation of these individual decisions will be the community's ultimate record of how it managed development.

By serving these three purposes, committed lands analysis provides some help with the problems identified in Chapter 2. Properly used, the techniques can help make planning advice current with what has actually occurred in the town, including bad land use decisions. The analysis will help developers argue for projects within the urban protectorate and can provide some solid factual basis for not allowing development in the urban frontier. Furthermore, if the analysis allows developers to choose sites appropriate for the projects they design, cooperation can emerge between planners and developers—the people whose expertise would ideally join to build the best future for a town.

The first principle of committed lands analysis is that because development patterns are determined by both public and private parties, a system devised to guide growth can succeed best if it is interjected into the decisionmaking processes of all these people. Local governments should encourage developers to choose among locations according to how much public fiscal benefit a project would bring. Private decisions are more likely to be made according to the premises of committed lands analysis if the town itself performs the calculations and publishes the results in a summary form. Using this summary, which could be available in city hall, the county courthouse, local banks, and realtors' offices, the developer could quickly calculate the net community benefit of alternative locations for a contemplated project.

GENERAL CONCEPTS FOR CALCULATIONS

Committed lands analysis measures the increased production efficiency achieved by bringing new customers to existing public facilities, and subtracts from that the additional cost of delivering services to those new customers. The discussion which follows will demonstrate how the formulas for measuring production efficiency and delivery costs have been derived.

Measuring Change in Production Efficiency

When the residents of a town undertake the construction of a capital facility, they are making an investment in that facility's capacity. As explained in Chapter 3, utilization of excess capacity can only increase efficiency in the production of public services, and for this reason committed lands analysis uses the existence of excess capacity as an indication that new customers can bring fiscal benefits to the community. The analysis assumes that the level of service, i.e., the quality of the water or the distance children are expected to walk to school, will remain unchanged after new customers arrive.

Committed lands analysis seeks to measure the change in production and delivery efficiency brought about by adding a new customer. Proper measurement requires a definition of customer that will allow comparisons among dissimilar developments; for example, between a large apartment building's production of wastewater and that of a single-family home. For this reason, the analysis establishes a standardized measure for utilization of public services, to be called the *standard customer*.[1] The formulas for calculating production efficiency are expressed in terms of standard customers. An example might illustrate this measuring device. A recent study in Montana found that a single-family house discharged 200 gallons of wastewater per day, while each unit of a multiple-family dwelling discharged 68 percent of that amount, or 136 gallons per unit. This means that when committed lands analysts estimate the effect of, say, a triplex on the production efficiency of a wastewater treatment plant, they would enter (3 × 0.68) or 2.04 as the "number of new customers" figure in the formula. If, on the other hand, they were estimating the effect of a single-family house, 1.0 would be entered as the number of additional customers.

Measuring change in efficiency is a complicated task, more complicated than most towns adopting committed lands analysis could easily undertake. For this reason, the analysis needs a simpler, more readily understandable surrogate measure for change in production efficiency. Remember the assumption underlying committed lands analysis: that a community builds public facilities with the intention of accommodating newcomers. Because efficiency will increase with the addition of new customers, and because per capita fiscal obligations for capital facilities will be reduced with the addition of new customers, committed lands analysis will equate the *cost reductions* brought by new customers with the *gain in efficiency* brought by new customers. That is, production efficiency is simply the cost savings brought by additional users of a capital facility with excess capacity.

In order to measure cost savings, costs for all types of services must be defined in a consistent way. The costs that are measured should only be those that are borne by the members of the community, meaning that any federal or state subsidies would not be included in the cost-saving analysis. In addition, measurement of costs must be designed so that the information is readily available and will remain constant within comparable time periods.

Taking these considerations into account, committed lands analysis will use the yearly budget for costs of current operations, maintenance, depreciation, replacement, and debt service. These are the yearly fixed obligations to operate a public facility, and these are the costs that new customers will share. Using the yearly fixed-cost obligation is a practical resolution to the complex problem of measuring cost savings brought by additional customers to different public facilities for two reasons. First, within each year, the existing capacity, level of service, and budget are rationally treated as fixed elements for the determination of costs borne by the community. Second, within each year, the budget pays for operations and debt service; as a result, the effects of changes to capacity of capital facilities will be reflected in yearly changes in debt service and operations budgets.[2] Furthermore, the discussion in Chapter 3 of the underlying economic model provides the assurance that these simplified measures have a well-grounded analytical basis.

Because the yearly budgets for each service will not vary as new customers are added—particularly in slow-growing jurisdictions for which committed lands analysis is intended—an additional customer will lower average costs by using existing excess capacity. Remember that excess capacity in a public asset is the precondition for committed lands analysis. Because additional users create the *possibility* for a reduction in average costs (and by extension tax rates, user rates, and mill levies), that potential reduction is here defined as the gain in production efficiency brought by growth. Since the yearly budget will be used as the basis of the efficiency calculations, a community would undertake committed lands analysis each year.

As long as excess capacity exists, the increased efficiency to be gained by adding new customers would be expressed, in its most simplified form, by Formula 1:

Formula 1. Gain in Production Efficiency

Term 1:   *Per Existing Customer Increase in Efficiency*
                Brought by New Customers

                          operate pub. fac.

$$\frac{\text{Yearly Fixed Obligation}}{\begin{array}{c}\text{Current Number of}\\\text{Customers}\end{array}} - \frac{\text{Yearly Fixed Obligation}}{\begin{array}{c}\text{Current Number + Additional Number}\\\text{of Customers} \qquad \text{of Customers}\end{array}}$$

Term 2   *Current Number of Customers*

Term 1 of this equation represents the per-existing customer
increase in efficiency that is caused by the addition of new
customers. When that gain in production efficiency is multiplied by
Term 2, the number of existing customers, the result is the net
increase in efficiency for the community brought by connecting
additional customers to an existing public facility.

Term 1 × Term 2 = *Community's Gain in Production Efficiency*
                            Brought by New Customers

A continuation of the wastewater treatment plant example from
Chapter 3 allows the practicalities of this formula to become clear.
Assume a wastewater treatment plant is capable of processing sewage
created by 1,000 houses, and assume that the community's yearly fixed
obligation for that plant's operation, maintenance, depreciation, replacement costs, and debt service total $1,000,000. If the plant were fully
utilized, its per customer obligation would be $1,000. If, however, only
500 houses were using the facility, each customer's obligation would be
$2,000, which means each is paying $1,000 for excess capacity. *Change in
production efficiency brought by an additional customer is the amount by which
an additional customer will reduce the yearly fixed obligation for the facility.* In
the simple case presented here, and using Formula 1 from above, adding
one new customer to the system will yield the following change in
efficiency:

$$\left(\frac{\$1,000,000}{500} - \frac{\$1,000,000}{501} \right) \times 500 = \begin{array}{l}\text{Community's Gain}\\\text{in Production}\\\text{Efficiency}\end{array}$$

$\$3.9921 \times 500 = \$1,996$

The above arithmetic shows that the addition of one new customer will yield $3.9921 in production efficiency for each existing customer. When that savings is multiplied by the number of existing customers (500 in this example), the total gain to the community is $1,996. Put another way, savings can be passed on to the existing 500 customers through a per-user reduction in bond payments collected to pay off the original investment in the oversized sewage treatment plant.

It should be noted that the closer to full utilization a capital facility comes, the smaller the efficiency gains brought by an additional customer. This is to be expected from the form of the production function graphs shown in Chapter 3, and from the fact that as the total number of customers increases, the denominators in the formula get larger while the investment in fixed capacity stays the same. Table 1, shown opposite, was derived simply by performing the simple arithmetic of Formula 1 for three different cases: first, when there were 500 original customers; second, when there were 750 original customers; and finally, when there were 999 original customers. (Note that the third case represents full capacity being reached when one additional customer is added.)

Graph A shows the value of gains in efficiency realized by adding a single customer at different capacity utilizations for the simple example used here:

Graph A

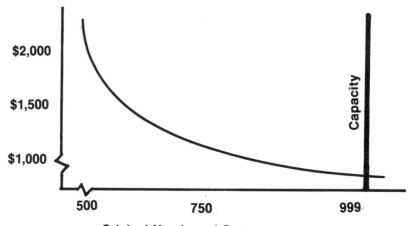

Original Number of Customers

These formulas will be applied to the case of an actual wastewater treatment plant in the case study section of this chapter.

When there are additional costs imposed by new customers, as in the case of a homeowner whose children must be bused to school, or a

Table 1. Community Gains in Production Efficiency

Original Number of Customers	Community's Gain in Production Efficiency
500	$1,996
750	1,332
999	1,000

commercial establishment for which a pumping station must be installed before it can be connected to the sewage treatment system, efficiency gains in production (i.e., cost savings) should be reduced by these user-specific costs. The following section discusses some appropriate reductions.

Measuring the Costs of Distribution

Communities build capital facilities to furnish services: schools provide education, sewage treatment plants clean wastewater, and so forth. An economist's definition of efficiency again guides the analysis: *providing what the public wants without wasting resources.* As explained in Chapter 3, committed lands analysis will assume "what the public wants" is reliably measured by the level of service delivery currently existing in a town.

The second part of the efficiency definition, "without wasting resources," refers to the actual cost considerations of providing services. Committed lands analysis will estimate, to the extent possible, the particular costs of delivery that are directly related to location of customers. For example, if a new subdivision is located beyond the current bus route for carrying children to the public school, the analytic method would estimate the additional costs of picking these children up so they can attend class. The cost of busing is the cost of delivering education, in the view of committed lands analysis.

Because a wastewater treatment plant is a collector system with a single point treatment plant, a user is connected to a sewer main so that gravity forces the effluent to reach the plant. While several research studies have both proven that collection costs for wastewater increase with distance from the customer and shown how these costs might be estimated, the analysis is more complicated than is practical for communities of the size for which committed lands analysis is intended.[3] Although the importance of such analysis cannot be ignored, its sophistication is unnecessary for relatively small, slow-growing communities. If in the future a simple measure is devised which can easily impute costs to distance, this section of the chapter can be revised. At this point we will simply assume that wastewater is efficiently collected from persons who connect to the treatment plant, and that the marginal cost of different locations is zero.

Net Community Benefit

For all the reasons discussed in Chapter 3, growth will clearly benefit a town if its location causes increased production efficiency without entailing delivery costs that exceed the value of that increased production efficiency. From this simple formulation, one can see that the net community benefit from new development can be measured as follows:

Community Gain in Production Efficiency − Cost of Delivering Services (if any) = Net Community Benefit from New Development

The terms of the simple subtraction formula clearly emphasize the importance of guiding growth within public facility service areas so as not to eat up gains in production efficiency realized from adding new customers.

HOW TO MAKE COMMITTED LANDS CALCULATIONS

The pages that follow offer a step-by-step description of how changes to production and distribution efficiency can be measured for a public wastewater treatment plant. Appendix A, the Calculation Appendix, will discuss similar measurements for public water supplies, public schools, and fire protection services. The attributes of each of these capital facilities differ from each other, meaning that the discussions appearing below and in the appendix can guide analysis of other major capital facilities.

Because committed lands analysis is new, local governments probably will have kept financial records without anticipating the specifics of this method. For that reason, proxy measures for individual pieces of information will be suggested, although these measures, too, may not exist in a municipality. In consultation with local officials, an analyst should devise measures that correspond to those used here. Such consultation will tailor committed lands analysis to an individual community's record-keeping standards. But in addition, it should enhance the analyst's working relationship with the administrators of public facilities and make the process of guiding growth more likely to be commonly accepted. One admonition must be offered: whatever measures are chosen must have a consistent mathematical and fiscal basis.

Case Study: Wastewater Treatment Plant

By working through the example of a wastewater treatment plant, the reader can come to appreciate the gains in efficiency brought by new customers using a facility with excess capacity. There are four sections in the case study:

1. Relevant Characteristics
2. Analysis of Efficiency
3. Result: Net Gain in Efficiency
4. Calculations

I. *Relevant Characteristics.* Committed lands analysis will determine the net benefit to the community from new customers being added to a public wastewater treatment system and will also ascribe a cost to the community from a new project being allowed to install a private septic system. The costs are based on the lost opportunity to increase production efficiency, although there are other, here unquantified, costs of private septic systems.

Private wastewater treatment systems (most frequently, septic systems) can be installed at little public expense, although private systems may contaminate the water supply and cause other environmental damage. While these external effects of private systems are well recognized, there is no generally accepted method for estimating their cost. Therefore, although the committed lands method recognizes these serious consequences, only opportunity cost will be used to measure the fiscal effects caused by decisions to install private septic systems. Opportunity cost represents the lost chance to increase production efficiency in a public sewage treatment plant that has available excess capacity.

II. *Analysis of Efficiency.* Committed lands analysis calculates the net gain in efficiency realized by serving new customers from an existing public facility. In order to make that final calculation, five determinations must first be made:

1. Common basis for defining a customer of each public asset;
2. Capacity and current utilization of each public asset, expressed in terms of customers;
3. Yearly fixed obligation for each public asset;

4. Change in production efficiency caused by new customers; and

5. Delivery costs that are related to the location of a customer.

Each of these are discussed below.

[Definition of Customers.]   A study referenced earlier in this chapter has shown that a single-family house discharges 200 gallons of wastewater per day. The analysis here will use that figure as the standard customer and express capacity and utilization of the wastewater treatment plant in terms of how many single-family houses it could accommodate.

[Capacity and Current Utilization.]   The analyst will define the capacity and current utilization of the wastewater treatment plant in terms of standard customers, i.e., single-family houses discharging 200 gallons of wastewater per day.

- Measurement of engineering capacity of the treatment plant in gallons per day that can be treated. This figure would be divided by 200—the discharge of a single-family house—to determine the capacity in terms of standard customers.
- Measurement of current use of the facility in gallons per day. This figure would be divided by 200 to determine the current utilization of the wastewater treatment plant in terms of standard customers.

To calculate available capacity, subtract the existing utilization in standard customers from the number of standard customers the plant is capable of processing. This is available unused capacity.

If a system is within 10 percent of its engineering capacity,[4] the required analysis is outside the scope of the committed lands method. In this case the costs of system expansion should be determined in consultation with the city engineer and with reference to a later section of this chapter, "Investment Decision for Assets Nearing Full Capacity."

[Yearly Fixed Obligations for the Wastewater Treatment Plant.]   Current budgetary obligations are the basis for measuring gains in production efficiency for the wastewater treatment system. These obligations are the current year's operations, maintenance, depreciation, replacement, and debt service costs that are paid out of sewer rates by the system's users. The way to determine the total obligation is to acquire a copy of the current budget for the wastewater treatment system and sum the expenditures for the items just listed. The total amount should be reduced by any federal or state subsidies for particular items.

[Efficient production of services.]   If there is excess capacity, it is possible to determine the gain in production efficiency brought by a new customer's hooking up to the existing wastewater treatment plant. The

formula for calculating change in production efficiency is repeated below:

$$\left\{ \frac{\text{Yearly Fixed Obligation}}{\begin{array}{c}\text{Current Standard}\\\text{Customers}\end{array}} - \frac{\text{Yearly Fixed Obligation}}{\begin{array}{c}\text{Current Standard}\\\text{Customers} + 1\end{array}} \right\} \times \begin{array}{c}\text{Number of}\\\text{Current Standard}\\\text{Customers}\end{array}$$

This formula is readily understandable. The addition of one standard customer will lower the average fixed cost of service to all existing users and leave the variable cost of service unchanged. This means that each user—new and old—will share the burden of the cost of sewage treatment. As long as there is excess capacity, committed lands analysis equates gains in production efficiency with the cost reductions that occur because costs are shared.

[*Efficient distribution of services*]   As explained earlier in this chapter, for wastewater treatment plants it is assumed that wastewater is efficiently collected from persons who connect to the treatment plant, and that the marginal cost of different locations is zero.

III. *Result: Net Gain in Efficiency.*   The calculation is simple: since there is no cost of distribution related to location, the net gain in efficiency is simply the change in production efficiency. This figure is the gain brought by each additional standard customer. If a proposed project were to encompass, say, ten standard customers, the net gain in efficiency would be the change in production efficiency multiplied by ten.[5]

IV. *Calculations.*   The following pages will illustrate how to calculate changes in efficiency resulting from new customers hooking up to the community's wastewater treatment system. The data comes from Missoula, Montana, and is representative of the experience of towns for which committed lands analysis was designed.

    1. The first step is to gather the data necessary for the analysis:

      a. Definition of customers

    Standard customers are measured by the amount of wastewater they produce. As described earlier, a standard customer is the equivalent of the 200 gallon per day (gpd, hereafter) volume created by a single-family dwelling.

      b. Capacity and Current Utilization—Information available from the city engineer

        i. 9,000,000 gpd capacity/200 = 45,000 standard customers

       ii. 6,000,000 gpd current use/200 = 30,000 standard customers

iii. The Missoula system is operating at 66.7 percent of capacity, and has available capacity for (3,000,000 gpd/200) or 15,000 additional standard customers.

c. Yearly fixed obligations for the wastewater treatment system $913,996 - Using the Missoula City budget, this is the total paid by taxpayers for operations, maintenance, depreciation, and debt service. This figure does not include state and federal revenue.

2. The second step is to make the necessary calculations. Using the data listed above, the change in efficiency is calculated as follows:

$$\left(\frac{\$913,996}{30,000} - \frac{\$913,996}{30,001} \right) \times 30,000$$

$$= (\$30.4665 - \$30.4655) \times 30,000$$

$$= \$.0010 \times 30,000 = \$30$$

This means that adding one standard customer to the system saves $.0010 per existing customer, and that the total reduction for the community in fixed cost burden is $30. If the community grew at a rate of 1 percent, this would mean that in the course of a year there could be a reduction in costs borne by existing customers amounting to $9,000.

3. Discussion. This measure of $30 system savings per standard customer is the base measure of efficiency gain used for comparison in committed lands analysis. First of all, it is the practical measure of committed lands: if the new customer located where no new collection mains have to be extended, the community will realize the total increase in efficiency of $30 per standard customer. At any other location, the net gain in efficiency will have to be reduced by the costs of extending services, as will be discussed in the section of this chapter entitled "Prudent Expansion of Committed Lands." This fact will allow comparisons to be made among different locations.

Second, this base measure allows the analyst to quantify the cost of allowing new customers to install their own septic systems. Without increasing variable costs, each potential customer could have saved the community a total of $30 in fixed cost burden. The committed lands analyst will consider this the opportunity cost to the community of not inducing a customer to connect to the public wastewater treatment plant. And finally, the $30 figure sets the upper limit on the value of inducements given to each potential customer (standard customer) to connect to the public system.

This section of Chapter 4 has demonstrated how the factors contained in the committed lands analysis formulas can be estimated. The reader interested in how the method could be altered to take into account different attributes of other major public assets is directed to Appendix A, the Calculation Appendix, where public schools, water systems, and fire protection services are discussed in detail.

HOW COMMITTED LANDS ANALYSIS CAN BE USED

The information derived from committed lands analysis can be used in three important ways. First, the calculations for different assets can be summarized so as to measure the relative advantages of new customers' locating within service districts with excess capacity. Second, the analysis will help public officials decide how to expand the geographic areas served by existing public facilities. And third, the analysis can help local governments decide where to locate new capital facilities when existing facilities reach full capacity.

Committed Lands Summary Sheet

To be successful, a system to guide growth must be used when developers are choosing locations. A local jurisdiction can encourage private decisions to be made according to the premises of committed lands analysis if the town itself performs the calculations and publishes the results in a summary form. Using this summary form—which could be available in city hall, the county courthouse, local banks, and realtors' offices—the developer could quickly calculate the net community benefit of alternative locations for a contemplated project.

The steps necessary to complete a committed lands summary sheet are three.

1. Identify each major public facility. For example, in Missoula County there are 13 elementary school districts, two high school districts, and three city fire districts.

2. Using the methods described in the case study, estimate excess capacity in terms of standard customers for each of these facilities.

3. Determine the net gain in efficiency an additional standard customer would bring. That is, calculate the effect of new customers on the production efficiency of each school district, wastewater treatment plant, public water supply, and the appropriate fire district. From each of these figures, the analyst will subtract any additional costs of delivering services to new customers. The result, then, will be the net change in community efficiency brought by an additional customer.

This figure is also the opportunity cost per standard customer caused by a choice *not* to use an available public facility. That opportunity cost can be referred to as the public cost of a private system.

The results of this summary could take the form suggested below:

Committed Lands Summary Sheet

	Capacity in Standard Customers	Efficiency per Additional Customer	Public Cost of Private System
Wastewater Treatment Plant:			
Facility 1:	_____	$_____	$_____
Facility 2:	_____	$_____	$_____
Public Water Supply:			
Facility 1:	_____	$_____	$_____
Facility 2:	_____	$_____	$_____
Fire Protection:			
District 1:	_____	$_____	$_____
District 2:	_____	$_____	$_____
District 3:	_____	$_____	$_____
Public Schools:			
District 1:	_____	$_____	$_____
District 2:	_____	$_____	$_____
District 3:	_____	$_____	$_____

Once this sheet is filled out, the committed lands analyst will have summarized for a community to what degree further development will result in gains in efficiency. A person looking at this summary sheet can see differences in gains from guiding growth into one service district or another.

Prudent Expansion of Committed Lands

Committed lands analysis can serve purposes other than evaluating sites for potential projects or evaluating a proposed project in terms of its public benefits. It can also help municipalities determine the location of new service areas for capital facilities with excess capacity and help decide whether it is fiscally prudent to connect new customers.

The first step in a decision about extending services is to estimate the increased production efficiency that a proposed project would bring. Using the methods described earlier, the analyst could calculate that value for each additional standard customer. The overall effect would be measured by multiplying this per standard customer value by the number of standard customers contained in a proposed project.

The next step is to determine how much it would cost to extend services to the new location. In most cases there are several methods of extension available, although topography may either limit the choices or require additional mechanical means. For example, pumping stations may have to be installed to deliver water to new customers located atop a relatively steep hill. This chapter cannot catalog the requirements for extending various services for all foreseeable locations of new development. Rather, the discussion will demonstrate by example how one might go about making a prudent decision.

Working with the city engineering office or the county surveyor, the analyst can determine the cost of each possible method of extending the particular service. For the public water supply, this could include the cost per foot of water mains, the cost per foot of trenching the main beneath bare ground and beneath asphalt, the acquisition cost of additional pumping stations or small reservoirs, and the cost of drilling a new well. The city engineer would doubtlessly prefer one method of extension as most suitable for the terrain and type of project. This process of determining the linear cost of service extension would be repeated for each public asset which would have to be expanded or improved in order for the proposed development to be served by existing public facilities.

The analyst would now have two figures. The first is the *maximum project gain,* which is simply the sum of added efficiency for each public service. The second is the *cost of extending services to the new development.* As long as the maximum project gain exceeds the cost of extending the service area, and assuming all other considerations argue for approving the project (the project complies with the comprehensive plan or the zoning regulations, for example), the committed lands analyst would recommend extending services.

Consider the following example as an illustration. Assume it has been shown that a project with ten standard customers would result in the following gain in efficiency:

Public Water Supply	$1,350
Wastewater Treatment Plant	300
Public Schools	2,999
City Fire District	1,870
Maximum Project Gain	$6,519

Assume also that while there is no public water main adjacent to the property, all other services are available at the location of the proposed project. Further assume the closest main is 150 feet away from the property line, so that the city would have to install a connection. After talking with the city engineer, the analyst determines that it will cost $29 per foot to install a properly sized main to serve the new project, or $4,350. That is, extending the main will result in a net gain for the community of $2,169 ($6,519 − $4,350).

The formula used in this last calculation (the total gain in efficiency less the cost of extending services to new customers) emphasizes a crucial point to committed land analysis: extensions to new customers should be carefully planned so that their cost does not eat up gains in production efficiency realized from adding those customers. Where a proposed project would show a net loss to the community, alternative sites should be considered in locations already served by other public services.

This discussion of expansion of committed lands may occur either because a developer requests approval for a project, or because tenants of existing structures ask to be connected to a public service. In either case, the calculations would be the same. Committed lands analysis suggests that decisions to extend a service to a particular location should always take into consideration other services already there, in as much as it will always be better to extend any single service into an area with the greatest number of other facilities with excess capacity. This consideration is fundamental to the aim of committed lands, which is to show how to achieve greater efficiency in public services in those places where

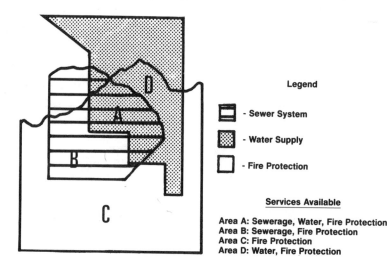

Legend

☐ - Sewer System

▨ - Water Supply

☐ - Fire Protection

Services Available

Area A: Sewerage, Water, Fire Protection
Area B: Sewerage, Fire Protection
Area C: Fire Protection
Area D: Water, Fire Protection

growth is relatively slow. The analysis takes existing characteristics of public capital facilities—where the plants are, their capacity, how services are provided—and attempts to improve their efficiency by directing the location of growth. This also means directing the location of new service areas so as to maximize efficiency in all public facilities. Using the methods in this chapter, a public official or a private developer can compare systematically the effects of distance and density (in terms of standard customers) on the public service budget of a community. Properly used, these comparisons can guide public decisions about where growth should be encouraged. They can also influence private decisions about where to develop projects that are justifiable in terms of their public fiscal benefits.

Investment Decisions for Assets Nearing Full Capacity

When existing public facilities approach the limits of their capacity, local governments must make extremely complicated decisions about major new investments in necessary capital assets. The effects of their choices will be felt by the community for years, not only because additional taxes must be levied to repay construction loans but also because the location of capital assets will influence the location of future growth. As one might expect, the literature of public administration and planning has a substantial amount of advice about how such decisions are best reached. These publications can be found under the rubric of *capital improvements planning*. The reader should look to this body of literature for guidance, with one additional consideration to be taken from committed lands analysis.

The interests of committed lands analysis are simply stated: because public investments exist that cannot easily be reduced, prudent public policy would have them used as efficiently as possible. As noted elsewhere in this chapter, it will always be better to build additional capital facilities in areas that have the greatest number of other facilities with excess capacity. The map that appeared in Chapter 3 is reproduced opposite to illustrate what committed lands analysis can contribute to a community's decision about building new capital facilities.

Assume that the sewage treatment system cannot clean a larger volume of wastewater, and community leaders decide that a new plant must be built. Committed lands analysis would interject the following consideration into the decision-making process regarding where that new plant should be located:

A decision to build the plant in area D, where there are both a public water supply and a fire protection system with excess available capacity, will result in a more efficient use of public assets than a decision to build in area C, where only fire protection services are available.

Committed lands analysis suggests that decisions about the location of a single capital investment should be made in the context of where services are available from other capital facilities.

NOTES

1. This is an adaptation of the surrogate measure suggested by the engineering firm of Brown and Caldwell for the city of Bozeman, Montana. Their measure, an "Equivalent Single-Family Dwelling Unit" or ESDU, calibrated wastewater volume and water consumption by different land uses according to how much a single-family dwelling unit would consume (in the case of fresh water) or produce (in the case of wastewater). The reader is referred to their report entitled "Feasibility of Implementing Annexation Fees and Utility Development Charges," October 1983. The report is available from Brown and Caldwell, Consulting Engineers; 28 Annette Park Drive; Bozeman, Montana 59715.

2. This approach is much more practical than the alternative of determining the present value of each set of long-term obligations for services where the time periods vary, meaning that the appropriate discount rates for different services would not be comparable.

3. See for example, Robert M. Clark and Richard G. Stevie, "A Water Supply Cost Model Incorporating Spatial Variables," *Land Economics* **57** (February 1981): 558–656, for a discussion of the regression analysis necessary.

4. If a public facility is operating with 10 percent of its capacity, there is ample time for a community to engage in planning to add to that capacity.

5. This is an approximation for small changes in the number of customers, and is recommended so that the analysis need only be done once a year. However, if a proposed project would bring a large number of new customers, the analysis should be made by using Formula 1 with the actual number of new customers, rather than simply multiplying the per customer change by the number of new customers.

5

Incentives for Guiding Development

Committed lands analysis has demonstrated that it makes fiscal good sense for local governments to guide growth to areas that have already been committed to development. Evidence of this commitment could be either excess capacity in capital facilities, or the ability to deliver public services more efficiently than is possible in outlying areas. Achieving growth in committed lands is the topic of the present analysis, and the methods that suggest themselves are perennial in their availability: sanctions and incentives. Sanctions, however, present numerous political and legal problems, especially where the ethic of autonomy in land use is strong. Incentives are the only practical corollary of committed lands analysis despite their infrequent use throughout the United States. One survey of urban growth management practices concluded: "Virtually all of the communities emphasize regulation or restraints. Very few systems incorporate or are considering incentives."[1] Committed lands analysis has given sufficiently good reason why local governments should undertake an active role in land management.

This chapter describes the steps that would be necessary to implement committed lands analysis in the local communities of Montana. The strategy and techniques are tied to Montana's political culture and legal framework. These political and legal features, though, are sufficiently common—for example, hostility toward bureaucratic regulation and fragmented administrative responsibility—that the Montana case study will offer pertinent guidance to local governments elsewhere that wish to try committed lands analysis. The chapter makes extensive use of interviews with both public officials and private parties involved in the development process. This method has two explanations. These are probably the most knowledgeable actors, and they are also indispensable players in any reform script. Engaging these interests is crucial to the success of committed lands analysis, as was argued early in this book, and this chapter emphasizes strongly that the very dynamics of the analysis encourage this result.

THE PRESENT REGULATORY SYSTEM

Land use regulation in Montana, as elsewhere in the nation, deals with such concerns as planning, zoning, subdivision permits, building permits, and the granting of variances. The purpose of planning is to determine what residents want for their community with respect to health, safety, welfare, the economy, and beauty. Zoning laws regulate such land use specifics as location and density of development. Subdivision regulation has the goal of securing safe and healthy development and proper allocation of the development's costs between the public and private sectors. Building permits are issued after local officials determine that there has been compliance with building codes. And variances are granted to prevent land use regulations from causing unreasonable hardships. A system of regulation that spells out procedures and assigns decisionmaking responsibility is necessary to put these land use policies into effect.

The local land use regulatory system in Montana has several key characteristics. First, there is a clear jurisdictional line separating counties and municipalities. County government, for the most part, has regulatory authority over the rural areas outside of municipal boundaries. Second, land use regulation is a shared responsibility of elected officials—the city council or county commission—and a planning office made up of a lay board and hired professionals. Third, the principal decisions affecting land use—zoning and subdivision regulation—are made pursuant to a two-hearing regulatory procedure. It is this two-step process that probably most characterizes land use regulation in Montana.

The two hearings are held before the planning board and the governing body. The chair of the planning board conducts the first hearing, and often a staff attorney is present to advise on procedural matters. The function of the first hearing is to listen to the testimony of the planning staff and balance their professional opinion against the concerns of citizens. The planning board's decision in the form of a recommendation is sent to the governing body, but, in fact, this first hearing is generally nothing more than a practice round for the second hearing before the elected officials.

The major reason why the second hearing is conducted *de novo* is that the county commissioners and city council members want to hear all of the testimony themselves because they have final decisionmaking responsibility. It is often the case that the second hearing before the city council is more politicized than the second hearing before the county commission. This is because the city council's smaller representative districts promote a ward mentality among the council members. The city council hearing also is generally more controversial than the county commission hearing because land development in the city is more likely to threaten the status quo of an established neighborhood in the urban protectorate. The city hearing process also can include another step, referral of the matters to a council committee for consideration and recommendation to the whole body. The committee can take up the issue at an open meeting and invite further public comment. Generally the committee's position carries considerable influence with the council.

When a land use proposal includes questions of both subdivision and zoning, the proceeding can be simplified rather than complicated. The ordinary way of handling such a request is to combine the issues at both hearing stages. Then the planning board and governing body each consider the zoning issue and the subdivision issue simultaneously. The hearing at each of the two stages could also include the third question of annexation.

The local board of adjustment becomes involved in land use regulation if the developer requests a zoning variance. The board of adjustment takes up this matter at a hearing prior to the other two hearings. The role of the board of adjustment is more prevalent in city land use regulation because city zoning ordinances tend to be not as flexible as county zoning law. The board of adjustment does not get involved in subdivision review.

There is disagreement among private developers and public officials about whom the two-hearing procedure favors. Developers often argue that the at-large citizenry benefits because the second hearing provides time to mobilize the public and marshall a vigorous protest against the presentations of professional consultants. Some government officials argue on the other hand that the advantage of two hearings is to the developer because professional consultants receive time to formulate arguments that refute the citizens' complaints. Despite their disagreement on this point, developers and public officials are in agreement that there is cause for discussion about reforming the present land use regulatory system.

REFORM ISSUES

Extended interviews with business leaders and public officials who are involved with land development and management in Montana indicate that there may be fertile ground in the state for one reform—a system of incentives for guiding growth.[2] Most of these people, whether their association with the present method of land use regulation is as a private citizen or a government official, can find fault easily and are frustrated by that system. The goal of any reform, as expressed by a business leader, should be "to put infill (i.e., committed lands) development on a competitive basis with outlying development."[3] The task of incentives would be to make development in areas of committed lands as easy as development in rural areas.

The most obvious and recurring explanation why there is so little infill development is the porous nature of Montana's subdivision regulations.[4] The occasional sale and family conveyance exceptions permitted by the Montana Code Annotated make rural development relatively regulation free.[5] In fact, 90 percent of the land subdivided in Missoula County has escaped local governmental review entirely. The reform approach to be discussed here, however, is not legislative revision of subdivision law. The 1987 Montana legislature demonstrated how difficult such a feat would be.[6] Rather, a system of incentives could be implemented locally and could make development within committed lands just as attractive as development under the exemptions.

Developers' frustrations with land regulation that turn them toward outlying areas are rooted in several experiences. One is the simple fact of comparative cost. A local government planning official observed that it ". . . is cheaper to build outside of the urban area because urban land is very expensive. Also, low density development in rural areas does not have to include expensive improvements such as curbs, gutters, and sidewalks."[7] The cost of development in urban areas can also be affected by the duration of regulatory procedures, while rural developers proceeding under the occasional sale and family conveyance exemptions can escape rigorous and extended scrutiny. The experience of one Missoula developer has been that the ". . . amount of time needed for review and approval is incredible for even a zoning change. This time, when related to interest rates, local economic conditions, and a short building season, can limit development greatly."[8]

Developers are also frustrated by the relative complexity, inflexibility, and politicization of land use regulation in urban areas. According to a high level city official, "the state's lax enforcement of its building code outside of the four and one-half mile limit"[9] prompts builders to escape the more rigorous enforcement of the city. The same result is achieved by the city's relatively inflexible zoning laws. While Missoula County zoning regulations, for example, expressly provide for conditional uses, developers in the city can achieve the same end only through a formal zoning change which invites an organized citizen protest and a resulting two-thirds council vote for approval. The obstacle presented by these complicated procedures is substantial because their potential for obstruction will be exploited by those opposing the change that development will bring to an established neighborhood. City council politics also drives developers to outlying areas. The ward representation system of city councils encourages ". . . councilmen to respond to narrow and short-run political pressures."[10] Council members, more than county commissioners, ". . . want to be able to help their constituents on land use matters."[11] The result is land use decisions turning on factional rather than broad and predictable considerations.

It is this final point that probably has caused the greatest frustration with the present land use regulatory system: the perception that the process is essentially unfair. The target of most criticism is the double hearing practice, one by the planning body and one by the governing body. More specifically, the target is the second hearing, the one conducted by elected officials. These hearing officers, as politicians, tend to be more swayed by presenters' sentiments than by legal criteria and the hearing record. The problem is that, in the words of a development professional, ". . . [v]ocal interests are motivated by narrow considerations, not community considerations."[12]

The conclusion that it is difficult to achieve objectivity and consistency in the second hearing is widely shared. A chamber of commerce official observes: "Uncertainty is getting worse; decisions should be based on fact, not hysteria."[13] This judgment is repeated by a city attorney ("Developers get abused under the current system because emotion and speculation control the final decision more than facts"),[14] a deputy county attorney ("Land use decisions can turn on purely emotional, speculative, and off-the-wall testimony"),[15] and a mayor ("The council listens to residents shouting down objective testimony contrary to their position").[16] The problems with a hearing conducted by elected officials can continue even after the hearing has supposedly been closed. *Ex parte* contact with the governing body, i.e., communication when only one party is present, appears to be frequent despite its illegality when the procedure is narrowly focused or quasi-judicial. One city official who has been a decisionmaker in such proceedings observes: "Once the hearing is closed, residents still work over the council members."[17]

This perception that it is difficult to receive a disinterested and objective hearing on land use issues causes some developers to react with a strategy of avoidance. Interviews with developers revealed that decisions by governing bodies over whether to allow or deny projects were frequently viewed as unpredictable. "This single fact causes developers to look for unzoned land, beyond the jurisdiction of local land use controls that they believe are wielded capriciously."[18] One suggested reform for attracting developers to committed lands is both politically and legally impossible: "removing the requirement for a public hearing."[19] What is possible, though, is reform of the hearing process to make it fair in fact and appearance. In the state of Washington, the supreme court was the agent of reform: "The development of the appearance of fairness doctrine in this state is closely tied to our recognition that restrictions on the free and unhampered use of property imposed by planning and zoning compel the highest public confidence in governmental processes bringing about such action."[20] On this point a commentator has noted: "The Washington Supreme Court created the appearance of fairness doctrine to maintain public confidence in the decisionmaking process of appointed and elected officials who decide the legal rights and privileges of parties after a public hearing."[21] The key aspects of the required fair hearing are "(1) the fairness of the hearing procedures and (2) the impartiality of the decision makers."[22] In Washington, local communities have met these requirements in land use proceedings by the employment of a hearing examiner. In Montana, the state supreme court has recognized "potential procedural problems in questions involving rezoning applications,"[23] but its ruling was far too weak to provide the reform impetus of the Washington decision. The push for reform in land use procedures in Montana, which could stimulate development in committed lands, will have to originate at the local government level.

Survey results are available that support the contention that the Montana public is in favor of creating some incentives to attract growth to committed lands. During the fall of 1987, the Bureau of Business and Economic Research at the University of Montana conducted an edition of its periodic Montana Poll. The Committed Lands Project contributed ten questions which were concerned with the attitudes of state residents about regulation of land development, encouraging development in already urbanized lands, and preference for living area.[24] Overall, the respondents to the poll demonstrated strong commitment to the following values: (1) the individual's right to develop property; (2) preservation of rural areas; (3) the individual's right to participate in land use regulatory procedures; (4) protection of the status quo in existing single family residence neighborhoods; and (5) preference for rural living. While some of these attitudes are in line with fostering committed lands development, some are potentially in opposition. The following discussion will attempt to reconcile the project's goals with the negative attitudes. Deserving of present emphasis, though, is the survey's findings that Montanans treasure open lands and that they are supportive of incentives to concentrate development in urban areas.

The high value Montanans place on their ability to enjoy rural settings is evident in the poll finding that 55 percent of the respondents favored a local government policy that would encourage "any new development to be located within the urbanized area rather than in the outlying area." Much of this disposition to guide growth was undoubtedly motivated by the central assumption of the committed lands project: sprawling development raises public costs. Over 68 percent of the survey respondents agreed that the "location of new development will affect the cost of the public services that your taxes pay for." The respondents also showed strong support for at least a financially based governmental incentive for influencing the location of growth. Sixty-four percent of the respondents agreed that a developer should get a "tax break" for building in an area committed to development. These responses indicate that the value of rural preservation and a desire for cost savings could be a sufficient popular foundation for a program of land management incentives.

There are grounds other than survey results for arguing that a favorable political climate for committed lands incentives exists. Interviews with persons active in the development community support the conclusion that this segment of the state's population would be strongly in favor of a system of incentives. All but one interviewee agreed that the location of development affects public costs although there is no method of passing development expenses on to the responsible parties. Several developers interviewed favored a system of committed lands analysis and incentives because they believed it would help them get a controversial project approved.

SUGGESTED INCENTIVES

The literature of local government management is quite suggestive of incentives that could be used to guide growth in committed lands.[25] The separate rationale of these incentives can be classified in three ways. First is the object of making development in committed lands less costly and more competitive with development in outlying areas. Second is the object of making development in committed lands easier in terms of meeting and modifying regulatory requirements. Third is the object of making the land use regulatory procedure for committed lands development as fair as possible in terms of its objectivity and predictability. These categories of rationale will be the basis of recommended incentives for stimulating development in committed lands to be discussed below. In each instance the incentives will have their own cost of implementation, and their utility will depend upon the benefits of committed lands development exceeding the cost of a package of specific incentives.

The virtue of the financial incentives is that they are easy to understand. They amount to a local government subsidy to committed lands development because citizens and officials believe that such development produces cost savings for the public. The most simple subsidy would be the assumption of certain development expenses by a local government. For example, general fund subsidies to builders in committed lands could include financial assistance for land improvements such as roads, sidewalks, curbs, and gutters. Other subsidies could include the costs of extending sewer or water mains to the development, utility hook-up and inspection fees, and such infrastructure contributions as a sewer development fee or donations for schools or parks.

Another kind of financial incentive would be a variation of the local government land bank. Some counties and municipalities in the United States have had the practice of acquiring land and managing growth by holding the land for open space or selling it for development. In Montana some communities, such as Bozeman and Missoula, have acquired land involuntarily.[26] These cities had sold tax-exempt, low-interest bonds to finance land improvements in private developments. When the developers went bankrupt, the cities were left with the responsibility of retiring the special improvement district bonds and ultimately became owners of the subdivision lots. The potential incentive for committed lands development that this situation gives rise to is the city's selling this land to developers at below market value. This incentive could, of course, be used with respect to other land held by the local government.

Property tax exemptions for new commercial and residential development within committed lands are another potential financial incentive. Montana cities presently have authority to grant tax exemptions based on a sliding scale for industrial development and for remodeled homes.[27] The state legislature could extend this property tax incentive to other kinds of development in committed lands on a temporary basis. The municipal redevelopment agency in Montana is another and an earlier example of a property tax based incentive for influencing urban development.[28]

A final financial incentive would be more indirect, consisting of increasing the cost of development in outlying areas rather than decreasing the cost of development in committed lands. Local governments could make it more expensive to build outside of the urban area by withholding public subsidies that were offered for committed lands development, imposing impact fees that represented the costs of development carried by the general public, and refusing to lend the government's bonding authority to special improvement districts. These measures, as is the case with the other financial incentives, have the purpose of making infill development look more attractive to the builder.

The second category of incentives for achieving committed lands development is facilitating the developer's use of the local government's land use regulatory process. Part of this approach would entail changes in governmental programs and regulatory procedures, but provision of this kind of incentive is also dependent on a change in the attitude of local government planners. Very simply, the local government employees who use their special training and experience to administer land use regulations should not have the status of an adversarial party. Rather, the planning staff should act more as an ombudsman or permit facilitator to expedite the permitting process. This regulatory posture was well described by a local government official: "Under a reformed regulatory system, the role of the planning staff should be analytical and objective, not an adversary of the applicant. The staff should help the applicant achieve his goals within the constraints of existing regulations."[29] One step in this direction would be to exclude the planning staff from the regulatory step of recommending a decision to the ultimate decision makers concerning committed lands development. The planning staff would make only a detailed evaluation of the developer's request.

Several changes in a local government's land use policies could be part of a system of regulatory incentives. To be effective, of course, these incentives could be made available only for committed lands development. Developers would be attracted by the opportunity, for example, to use a sharply abbreviated review process for minor developments; to have an extended period of time during which an authorized permit would be effective; to have the planning staff authorized to make minor changes in permits after the permits are granted; and to have the local government bear the burden of proving noncompliance with criteria in a land use regulatory proceeding.

Other policy changes that would constitute an incentive would at least equalize the regulatory ease of committed lands development and outlying development. For example, rural development would be less attractive if county government were to insist on strict building code enforcement outside of the four and one-half mile urban penumbra and require smaller building lots in outlying areas so that on-site sewer and water facilities would be precluded. Probably most importantly, urban development would be fostered if city zoning regulations were as flexible as county zoning regulations. The city's, like the county's, use of special exception and conditional use zoning would allow builders in committed lands to enjoy certain regulatory exceptions that were stated in the ordinance. For example, a builder would qualify for special consideration concerning building height, density, and improvements on the condition of locating the development in the city's committed lands. A special exception in a zoning ordinance would permit mobile homes, apartment houses, or neighborhood businesses solely because of their location in committed lands. An approach similar to incentive zoning for guiding growth is granting bonus points for building in committed lands when a permit system based on points is being used.[30] The attraction to the developer would be similar to the incentive created by conditional use zoning. Because of the extra points gained from building in committed lands, less stringent regulatory compliance would be needed for such development features as building height and density as well as site improvements.

Outright waivers of regulatory requirements could also be part of an incentive system tied to regulations. A local government could waive or reduce property improvement requirements (e.g., curb, gutter, sidewalk, and road) for developments in committed lands. Further, the local government could allow the property improvements that were required to be phased in according to market demand for building sites. Other waivers could include dedication of park lands and permit requirements such as for tree removal or an excavation.

One final adjustment in municipal regulatory policy could result in the creation of a significant incentive. A city could adopt a liberal contract policy for extending municipal services to the urban area beyond the city limits. The theory is that builders would locate in these committed lands if sewer, water, emergency services, improved police protection, and road maintenance were readily available. In cities like Missoula, where protection of the community's aquifer is of primary importance, an urban sewer service district would be an especially powerful incentive for committed lands development. The policy could be acceptable to the city council because it would provide "leverage for annexation, protection of ground water, and reduction of service costs in the long run."[31] A Missoula business leader has said: "The best thing the city could do to promote infill development is to extend sewer service to the urban area outside of the city limits."[32] And a development consultant has similarly concluded that the city council's "policy on contract sewer is the single-most effective land use tool in this community."[33]

The third category of incentives for achieving committed lands development deals with procedural matters. The principal reform and the source of contemplated benefits is substitution of a hearing examiner system for the present regulatory process of two hearings, one conducted by a planning commission and the second conducted by the locally elected governing body. The argument is that this change is capable of meeting criticism from developers that the present system is lacking in predictability and objectivity. If local governments were to provide a hearing process administered by a hearing examiner for regulation in committed lands, then developers would be more likely to choose that location over outlying areas.

The critical issue about the hearing examiner system is whether its design and procedures can answer the criticisms of developers in a manner that the public will judge to be fully fair and democratic. The state of Washington, which is in the forefront of eight states[34] that have authorized the use of hearing examiners for land use regulation, has concluded that the hearing examiner system has met this challenge.[35] The reform was adopted by Washington local governments in the late 1970s because there was a generally perceived lack of fairness in the conduct of land use regulatory hearings by planning commissions and local governing bodies. All parties involved—applicant, the public, and the planning staff—had felt that the procedures were too informal, decisions were being based on political considerations and information not in the record, and the decisions themselves were arbitrary and highly unpredictable. The hearing examiner reform substituted a hearing format characterized by functional informality, professional objectivity, and carefully reasoned decisions. There is broad agreement among all interested parties that the purpose of the reform, as set out in the Community Development Guide of Redmond, Washington, has been realized: "The purpose of the hearing examiner system is to separate the application of land use regulations from planning and policymaking; to provide a level of expertise to conduct administrative and quasi-judicial hearings arising from the application of the development guide and the rules and procedures developed under it; to better protect and promote the interests of the community; and to expand the principles of fairness and due process in public hearings."

The essential features of the hearing examiner reform proposal are few and simple.[36] The hearing examiner, whose job would be to preside at hearings concerning land use in committed lands, could be an attorney or nonattorney and could be a government employee or retained by contract. The hearing examiner's decisions could either be final, or they could consist of recommendations to the governing body in the form of findings of fact, conclusions of law, and proposed resolution. Appeals to the governing body, should the hearing examiner's decisions be final, could be dealt with by the governing body summarily or *de novo.* The status of the hearing examiner's decisions and the nature of the appeals procedure could vary from jurisdiction to jurisdiction and within a jurisdiction according to the kind of land use proceeding.

The success of implementing the hearing examiner reform in Montana would seem to depend most of all on education of the public about the operation of the system and on the abilities and attitudes of the hearing examiner. It would be absolutely essential for the hearing examiner, in a prefatory statement at the hearing, to tell those present about the issues at stake and the procedure to be used. This emphasis on public understanding would previously have been observed through the generous posting and advertising of notice of the hearing; by making the applicant's file available as well as sending it out to those who request it; and by making available the planning department's report in advance of the hearing so that the public can respond to it during the hearing. Public understanding and confidence would also be enhanced because the hearing examiner's decision would be grounded in the hearing record and explained in a reasoned opinion.

The way the hearing examiner conducts the hearing is also critical for the public's judgment that it is a democratic forum. A prehearing conference, which could include a representative of a neighborhood group, would be used to mediate preliminary conflicts between interested parties and to structure the hearing. To put the public at ease, the hearing format would be narrative and not adjudicatory. Questions by the hearing examiner and not cross-examination conducted by counsel would be used to build a complete record and get information to the public. The hearing examiner would welcome questions from the audience and use them to structure the hearing. An atmosphere of openness would be preserved by the hearing examiner's ordinarily placing no restrictions on the length and content of testimony, although repetitive and extraneous remarks would be eliminated in the final report. The hearing examiner, however, would be careful to maintain an atmosphere of propriety and fact finding, and would use threats of sanctions to control the audience. Also, the hearing examiner's strict adherence to the *ex parte* rule would assure the public that the hearing, and not informal conversations and emotion, were the basis of the decision. The hearing examiner would take matters under advisement, deciding within a stated number of days rather than on the spot. Finally, the governing body's right to hear an appeal or make the final decision would assure the public that elected officials would review a recommended decision and remedy errors.

The hearing examiner system is capable of generating a broad base of support, even though the reform would likely consist of one land use hearing conducted by an unelected official. The general public's acceptance of the system would result from the hearing examiner's commitment to democratic values and professional responsibility to implement objectively the policy of the governing body. Acceptance of the system by developers would result from the on-the-record proceeding, the single-hearing format, the strict adherence to a published hearing schedule, and the hearing examiner's lack of personal interest. Planning staff's acceptance of the system would result from their removal from making final decisions on hot issues, their gaining more time for critical research tasks, and their increased policy guidance because of the hearing officer's reasoned decisions. The argument in the context of the committed lands project is that these benefits are so significant that the reform's implementation for committed lands would stimulate development in those areas.

OBSTACLES TO IMPLEMENTATION

The attractiveness of committed lands analysis and the incentives for achieving its benefits should not blind local government officials to obstacles that stand in the way of implementation. These are both legal and political and should not be underestimated as serious roadblocks. Attitudes about the use and regulation of private property are deeply held. The Montana Poll (cited above) found that 68.6 percent of those questioned agreed either "strongly" or "somewhat" that an "individual's right to develop his property is generally more important than the public's interest in having that right regulated by the government." The likely categories of opponents of committed lands incentives—those against using public money to guide growth and those in favor of traditional residential neighborhoods, rural living, and multiple land use hearings—are certain to use any available political and legal leverage to block the reforms.

There does exist in Montana law a sound but probably not fully adequate basis for the incentives to build in committed lands. The legislative powers of a municipality include, for example, the duty to "secure and promote the general public health and welfare."[37] The state subdivision law authorizes every local government to adopt regulations "for the avoidance of subdivisions which would . . . necessitate an excessive expenditure of public funds for the supply of [public] services."[38] And the legislative authorization for local government planning instructs each county and municipality "to improve the present health, safety, convenience, and welfare of their citizens and to plan for the future development of their communities to the end that . . . new community centers grow only with adequate highway, utility, health, educational, and recreational facilities; . . . and that the growth of the community be commensurate with and promotive of the efficient and economical use of public funds."[39] Should a county lack clear authorization to act and a municipality be properly empowered, an interlocal agreement between these units could enable the county to proceed: "Any one or more public agencies may contract with any one or more other public agencies to perform any administrative service, activity or undertaking which any of said public agencies entering into the contract is authorized by law to perform."[40]

These general authorizations are supplemented by more specific provisions that are related to specific committed lands incentives. Montana statutes allow municipalities to "impose a special assessment reasonably related to the cost of any special service or special benefit provided by the municipality or impose a fee for the provision of a service,"[41] and municipal practice has included suspension of fees as well as waiving permits and using gas tax money to pay for land improvements in private developments.[42] Montana law also authorizes cities and towns to furnish water and sewer services to persons located outside of the municipality at rates that are "reasonable" and approved by the Public Service Commission.[43]

Montana law appears to authorize sufficient flexibility in zoning requirements to permit committed lands incentives based upon special zoning conditions or exceptions. For example, the municipal zoning law establishes the purpose of zoning as "promoting health, safety, morals, or the general welfare of the community,"[44] and then allows the governing body to "divide the municipality into districts of such number, shape, and area as may be deemed best suited to carry out the purposes of this part."[45] Zoning districts that would encompass committed lands should have no trouble escaping the state supreme court's prohibition of spot zoning. In *Little* v. *Board of County Commissioners of Flathead County*[46] the court defined spot zoning in a way that would exclude incentive zoning for committed lands:

Generally, . . . three factors enter into determining whether spot zoning exists. . . . First, . . . the requested use is significantly different from the prevailing use in the area. Second, the area in which the requested use is to apply is rather small. This test, however, is concerned more with the number of separate landowners benefited by the requested change than it is with the actual size of the area benefited. Third, the requested change is more in the nature of special legislation. In other words, it is designed to benefit only one or a few landowners at the expense of the surrounding landowners or the general public.

Another likely legal challenge to zoning that would allow special exceptions in districts defined by committed lands would be based on equal protection analysis.[47] Residents from elsewhere in the local government jurisdiction would argue that they were the objects of discrimination: that they did not have available to them the same benefits and advantages as those in committed lands. There seems to be little doubt that incentive zoning "stands a better chance of meeting constitutional requirements if it complements a rational underlying regulation and represents a reasonable means of achieving a permissible government objective."[48] Committed lands analysis and concern for governmental efficiency certainly would supply this necessary rational basis. Reviewing the legality of a variety of growth control techniques, one study found that they would "be valid only if they can be related to the police power through their tendency to serve the general welfare. . . . In a general constitutional attack, once the objective is found to be legitimate, the courts decide whether the means employed are reasonably related to the objective."[49]

The basis in Montana law for the committed lands incentive consisting of a single land use hearing conducted by a hearing examiner is more certain for municipalities than for counties. For subdivision regulation, the state code clearly authorizes both cities and counties to use a hearing examiner and one hearing: "The governing body or its authorized agent or agency shall hold a public hearing on the preliminary plat. . . . When a hearing is held by an agent or agency designated by the governing body, the agent or agency shall act in an advisory capacity and recommend to the governing body the approval, conditional approval, or disapproval of the plat."[50] Municipalities, however, are given by the code a broad authorization to use a hearing examiner which would extend to all kinds of land use hearings: "Except for budget hearings, the governing body may designate a subcommittee or hearing examiner to conduct public hearings."[51] For both counties and municipalities, action on zoning regulations appears to require two hearings, one by the planning board and one by the governing body.[52]

A credible constitutional challenge to the committed lands incentive of a single hearing conducted by a hearing examiner is unlikely. Due process simply requires that no changes in a person's liberty or property interests be officially considered except after adequate notice and a fair public hearing. In fact, it was the Washington Supreme Court's doubt that a fair hearing could be provided by local boards and commissions that led to that state's adoption of the hearing examiner system.[53] The Oregon Supreme Court subsequently raised the same questions, inquiring whether a local legislative body met the exacting due process requirements of a rezoning proceeding, a quasi-judicial matter in that court's eyes.[54] The Idaho Supreme Court too has held that rezoning requires special attention to safeguarding due process rights: "We are persuaded the cases which characterize as quasi-judicial the action of a zoning body in applying general rules or policies to specific individuals, interests, or situations represent the better rule."[55] The Montana Supreme Court, however, is not part of this trend. While it would not fault the basic design of a hearing examiner system from a due process perspective, it also would not find the present rezoning hearing system so deficient as to require a hearing examiner. In 1979 the Montana Court said: "A rezoning ordinance, like a zoning ordinance, is a legislative enactment, and is entitled to the presumptions of validity and reasonableness."[56]

Interviews with local officials make it clear that political obstacles to implementing the committed lands incentives are more formidable than the legal obstacles. The city council or county commission could lack sufficient motivation to act. To the elected politicians, the public cost savings predicted by committed lands analysis could appear to be too vague and speculative. They could view the role of the hearing examiner as a threat to their governing power and as diminishment of their political opportunities. It would be the hearing examiner and not the council members or commissioners who would preside at public and highly visible forums and who would formulate the outlines of the decisions. The elected officials might not want to defend themselves against charges that they restricted their constituents' opportunity to participate in land use regulatory decisions.[57] And the politicians might believe that the present land use regulatory system is best because its looseness and informality allow weighing of all relevant opinions and because it promotes workable and acceptable compromises through a prolonged give and take.[58]

The greatest political obstacles stem from the extremely conflictive nature of land use politics among the public. People feel deeply about their freedom to use their land, choose their dwelling place, and protect the integrity of their neighborhood. The committed lands project's survey of Montanans found that only 15 percent of the respondents "strongly" supported locating apartment buildings and mobile homes closer to single-family houses in order to decrease the costs of public services. The survey also found that many Montanans would insist on being able to build or live in outlying areas. Twenty-nine percent of the respondents desired a more rural residence in the state, and a 36.3 percent plurality of the respondents said that "open space" would be the critical factor if they "could live wherever they wanted in their county." These findings arguably forebode poorly for the success of policies that would discourage rural development and encourage a mixture of development on the vacant land in traditional single-family neighbor-hoods. The dimension of the political obstacle becomes clear when it is remembered that threatened neighborhoods organize effectively and that ward politicians are prone to serve their constituents' demands.

Much of the politicization that would surround the policy of commit-ted lands incentives could be pre-empted if a comprehensive city/county land use plan were previously adopted. Adoption of a master plan would have depended on achieving consensus among disparate elements of the community: rural and urban residents, the various neighborhoods, and city and county officials. The master plan would represent agreement, rather than continuing strife, over such issues as where development is suitable, where development is desirable, and what kind of development is permitted. Absence of a master plan would mean that each use of a committed lands incentive could be accompa-nied by a bitter political debate over fundamental questions of growth.

The absence of an up-to-date comprehensive land use plan, then, is a good sign that the community is lacking a consensus for reform. Implementation of committed lands incentives would be considerably more difficult. There would be less likelihood of the county government forbearing when the city government was adopting incentives to attract development to its precincts.[59] It would be less likely that the public would view the hearing examiner as an agent of the policymaking body and more likely that the hearing examiner would be viewed as an autonomous bureaucrat with substantial decisionmaking discretion. There would be less likelihood that the granting of regulatory exceptions would be seen as a protection of the public interest and more likelihood that incentives would be viewed as selective and susceptible to political manipulation. Without a master plan, the flexibility of the incentive system could become its fatal flaw rather than its virtue.

The conclusion is not necessarily that a revised master plan is absolutely essential to a program of guiding growth from the perspective of the committed lands concept. A substitute for the master plan could be the community's going through the committed lands analysis itself, and its immersion into the empirical findings and formulation of suitable incentives. Done in the right way—with broad participation, gradual evolution of policy, and strong leadership—the insights and conviction gained from committed lands analysis could serve as the needed foundation of consensus for the incentive program. The public's shared judgment that there were cost savings to be realized and that the incentive system was democratic and in the public interest then could be sufficient offsets to the countervailing notion that development decisions are purely a private matter.

NOTES

1. American Society of Planning Officials, *Urban Growth Management Systems*, The American Society of Planning Officials Press, Reports No. 309 and 310 (no date), p. v.

2. See Appendix B, the "Survey of the Development Community," for a summary of the results of these extended interviews.

3. Interview with David Owen, executive director, Missoula Chamber of Commerce, August 7, 1987.

4. Interview with Joan B. Newman, deputy county attorney for Missoula County, August 13, 1987.

5. *Montana Code Annotated*, 76-3-207.

6. The Fiftieth Session of the Montana legislature killed HB 809 in committee, a measure put forward by the Montana Environmental Quality Council to reform extensively the state's present subdivision law. According to Richard Weddle, department of commerce attorney, in a March 24, 1988, telephone interview, developers and planners could not agree on reforms in the law's public interest criteria and regulatory exemptions.

7. Interview with Paula Jacques, Missoula city/county planner, July 22, 1987.

8. Interview with Nick Kaufman, land development consultant, July 24, 1987.

9. Interview with Robert Lovegrove, mayor of Missoula, July 29, 1987.

10. Kaufman interview.

11. Interview with Jim Nugent, Missoula city attorney, July 28, 1987.

12. Kaufman interview.

13. Owen interview.

14. Nugent interview.

15. Newman interview.

16. Lovegrove interview.

17. Lovegrove interview.

18. Committed Lands Project, "Detailed Survey Results," (no date), p. 5.

19. Kaufman interview.

20. *Narrowsview Preservation Association* v. *City of Tacoma*, 526 P. 2d 897, 900 (1974).

21. Carolyn M. VanNoy, "The Appearance of Fairness Doctrine: A Conflict in Values," *Washington Law Review* **61**: 2 (April 1986): 533.

22. *Ibid.,* p. 545.

23. *Foster* v. *City of Bozeman,* 614 P. 2d 1072, 1078 (1980).

24. Appendix C, the "Results of the Montana Poll," summarizes the results.

25. See, for example, David J. Brower, Candace Carraway, Thomas Pollard, and C. Luther Propst, *Managing Development in Small Towns* (Chicago: American Planning Association Press, 1984); Michael J. Meshenberg, *The Administration of Flexible Zoning Techniques* (Chicago: American Society of Planning Officials Press, 1976); American Society of Planning Officials, *Urban Growth Management Systems,* (Chicago: ASPO Press, (no date); Stephen M. Smith, Gerald E. Marousek, and Don Blayney, "Managing the Costs of Growth in Rural Communities in the 1980s," *State and Local Government Review* **16:** 3 (Fall 1984): 130–135; John Vranicar, Welford Sanders, and David Mosena, *Streamlining Land Use Regulation* (Chicago: American Planning Association, 1982); Timothy Beatley, "Ethical Issues in the Use of Impact Fees to Finance Community Growth," paper presented at the New York annual convention of the American Planning Association, April 25, 1987; and Nels R. Leutwiler, "Playing Taps for Urban Growth Control: Restricting Public Utility Access to Manage Growth," *State and Local Government Review* **19:** 1 (Winter 1987): 8–14.

26. See *Great Falls Tribune,* August 4, 1986.

27. *Montana Code Annotated,* 15-24-1401, 1501.

28. See *Montana Code Annotated* Title 7, Part 42, especially 7-15-4234.

29. Lovegrove interview.

30. An example of a regulatory system using points is the city of Missoula's "Reserve Street Development Packet."

31. Interview with Bruce Bender, city of Missoula assistant engineer, August 14, 1987.

32. Owen interview.

33. Kaufman interview.

34. These eight states are Arizona, California, Florida, Illinois, Maryland, Ohio, Oregon, and Washington.

35. The authorization for the state of Washington's hearing examiner system is *Revised Code of Washington Annotated,* Titles 35 and 35A. The opinions about the nature and success of the Washington hearing examiner system come from interviews with James Driscoll, hearing examiner for Redmond, Edmonds, and Everett; Duane Bowman, Edmonds planning director; Dennis Derrickson, Everett planning director; Gerry Ervine, Everett senior planner; and John Galt, Snohomish County hearing examiner.

36. See Appendix D, "Outline of Rules of Procedure for Proceedings before a Hearing Examiner," for a summary of the contents of an implementing ordinance.

37. *Montana Code Annotated,* 7-1-4123(2).

38. *Montana Code Annotated,* 76-3-501.

39. *Montana Code Annotated,* 76-1-102(1).

40. *Montana Code Annotated,* 7-11-104.

41. *Montana Code Annotated,* 7-1-4123(7).

42. Nugent interview.

43. *Montana Code Annotated,* 7-13-4312.

44. *Montana Code Annotated,* 76-2-301.

45. *Montana Code Annotated,* 76-2-302.

46. 631 P. 2d 1282, 1289 (1981).

47. For a general discussion of trends in land use law see David R. Godschalk, David J. Brower, Larry D. McBennett, and Barbara A. Vestal, *Constitutional Issues of Growth Management* (Chicago: ASPO Press, 1977); Robert H. Freilich, David S. Frye, and Dianne T. Carpenter, "The New Federalism—American Urban Policy in the 1980s: Trends and Directions in Urban, State, and Local Government Law," *The Urban Lawyer* **15:** 1 (Winter 1983): 159–231; and Edith Netter (ed.), *Land Use Law: Issues for the Eighties,* Part II (Chicago: Planners Press, 1984).

48. Brower, *Managing Development*, p. 106.

49. *Urban Growth Management Systems,* pp. 60–61.

50. *Montana Code Annotated,* 76-3-605(1) and (4).

51. *Montana Code Annotated,* 7-1-4131(6).

52. *Montana Code Annotated,* 76-2-205 and 76-2-307.

53. *Smith* v. *Skagit County,* 453 P. 2d 832 (1969).

54. *Fasano* v. *Board of County Commis*

sioners of Washington County, 507 P. 2d 23 (1973).

55. *Cooper* v. *Board of County Commissioners of Ada County,* 614 P. 2d 947, 950 (1980).

56. *Schanz* v. *City of Billings,* 597 P. 2d 67, 71 (1979).

57. Interview with Ann Mary Dussault, Missoula County commissioner, August 4, 1987.

58. Newman interview.

59. Dussault interview.

6

Conclusions: Productive Planning

When a town changes in ways that seem ugly or disagreeable, when elected officials make decisions that unfairly favor certain groups at the expense of others, and when taxes rise without any improvement in public services, citizens understandably become disheartened about the way public affairs are conducted. Planners, especially, become downcast when their efforts to forestall problems go unheeded as often as not. This book speaks to these discouraged citizens and planners. Early chapters described the mechanics of land use decisionmaking as they actually operate, and subsequent chapters introduced committed lands analysis as a means of squaring these mechanics with the aims of planning by joining public and private interests in development. Committed lands analysis can be used as it appears here, or the philosophy that inspired this method of guiding growth can serve as a model for confronting fundamental disabilities of local planning practice.

FUNDAMENTAL REALITIES

The reality of local land use decisions is easy to summarize. In deciding whether to allow a proposed development on a particular site, elected officials tend to respond to their constituents' emotional appeals and to short-run budget pressures. Officials will agree with a neighborhood's desires to be protected from what it regards as an undesirable project no matter how necessary that development is to the community; they will allow random development of vacant fields where public services will be needed but do not yet extend; and they will ignore planners' sound advice when it runs contrary to the wishes of politically powerful adversaries.

Planners face a fundamental problem when they try to enlist popular support to overcome these practical realities. Most citizens can see the need for planning when it has been absent or when a crisis develops, but they ordinarily take successful planning for granted because it circumvents problems before they occur. People are pleased that their children have safe playgrounds close by, that shopping is convenient to their houses, and that landscaping softens the brash outlines of commercial strip development. However, citizens are more likely to think these attributes are simply the way things should be than to realize they result from successful planning. Hence, planners who wait for public support on a contested issue usually wait in vain. These are the simple facts of local land use decisionmaking.

Also easy to summarize are the reasons that planning staffs are ignored in the process of land use regulation, even though they have been hired to help make those decisions. State codes almost without exception describe the purpose of local planning in compelling language:

> . . . It is the planning department's objective to improve the present health, safety, convenience, and welfare of all citizens and to plan for the future development of the community by assuring that highway systems be carefully planned; that new community centers grow only with adequate highway, utility, health, educational and recreational facilities; that the needs of agriculture, industry and business be recognized in future growth; that residential areas provide healthy and desirable surroundings for family life; and that the growth of the community be commensurate with and promotive of the efficient and economical use of public funds.[1]

Although this authorization is a valid statement of the planning function, it will seem abstract and unconvincing to elected officials who are confronted by the political power of a neighborhood delegation opposing the planning staff's support of an apartment building, or by a developer's promise of new construction jobs and property tax revenue from a project the planning staff opposes. To citizens, landowners and elected officials, the principles of planning often seem a mire of conflicting and competing axioms.

Successful planners realize that their statutory mandate succeeds through a series of small decisions; for example, zoning regulations that require grass and shade trees in front of each new structure will, over time, result in a well-landscaped town. However, this patient faith in implementing zoning requirements will not check the developer's vehement argument that landscaping requirements are so costly as to prevent a project's being built. Indeed, because they know that officials share some of their reservations about planning, developers and land-owners do not make planning an integral part of their decisions about where to locate and how to design projects. The ultimate effect is that planners are consulted only after developers have chosen a parcel and drawn up site plans. At this point, planners can at best effect small modifications in the development not only because their reviewing time is limited by law once a proposal is submitted, but also because developers become understandably reluctant to redesign projects thoroughly or consider alternate sites once money has been spent on a proposal. Compounding the weakness of planners is the fact that elected officials, absent strong and informed public support for the planners' concerns, will avoid controversy and vote with the developer or with an apparently unified neighborhood demanding protection from an unwanted land use. In effect, the considerations of the local planning staff are tangential to developers who choose sites and design projects, to elected officials who must approve building projects, and even to the public who will ultimately live in new developments.

Any effort to reform land use decisions must be responsive to these well known weaknesses in the land use decisionmaking process. Planning will become effective if consequences of incremental decisions can be made unmistakable, and if the rationale for planning can be argued in readily understood and compelling terms. Most importantly, planners will have a significant effect only if their concerns come to be inextricably entwined in the decision-making processes of all people—public officials and private entrepreneurs alike—whose actions affect land development. Because no single reform can prevent the recurrence of all bad land use decisions that have been made, a reform effort should choose a set of problems and concentrate on their solution.

COMMITTED LANDS ANALYSIS

The authors have identified a set of contemporary land use problems that can be solved by a more efficient use of public assets. These problems occur because development projects do not get approval easily in the urban protectorate, causing developers to choose sites on the urban frontier. When elected officials approve these projects on the outskirts of town, they rarely give serious consideration to public service costs that might result from spread-out patterns of growth. Committed lands analysis has been designed as a method to solve this set of problems.

Committed lands analysis is an effective tool because it is easy to understand, simple to use, and persuasive at public hearings. Rather than relying on rigid governmental procedures to inform land use decisions, committed lands analysis influences the early land use planning of private developers. Its attraction is its highly visible method of measuring the public benefits of a project, which later can provide a compelling argument in the formal regulatory process. In this way, committed lands analysis can overcome several disabling realities of local land use decisionmaking.

Because the cost of providing services falls as the utilization of public facilities increases, committed lands analysis encourages growth within the service areas of existing facilities. The budget becomes the point at which public and private interests meet, and makes unmistakably clear the crucial connection between land development and the cost of public services. Committed lands analysis makes a town accountable for its decisions: even if officials choose to allow development where no public efficiency can be gained, everyone knows the cost of that decision.

Committed lands analysis is an effective planning method because it makes good practical sense. The method offers fiscal prudence as a rationale for developers' choosing sites and arguing for approval of projects located there. In the urban protectorate, this rationale can counter a neighborhood's emotional objections by making clear the public cost of keeping individual areas homogeneously built. This cost has not been clear before. In the urban frontier, where there is little guidance for development choices, the method offers a way of choosing where development should go. This factual basis, too, has been lacking.

By using committed lands analysis, planners can convince developers and elected officials that guiding growth can result in public assets being used more efficiently. Using the arguments the analysis provides, developers will choose sites in the urban protectorate, not the urban frontier, because they are more likely than heretofore to convince elected officials to approve their projects over a neighborhood's protest.

And finally, the authors realize that few people refute the commonsense tenets of planning. It is the individualized application of planning

—its regulatory aspect—that engenders hostility and that causes inappropriate pressures to be brought to bear on decisionmakers. The hearing examiner system recommended earlier would alleviate much of this discord, properly channel community pressure, and leave the planning board and local governments free to define in a responsible way the broad interest of the community.

The authors have urged slowly growing towns with large investments in under-used capital facilities to consider the methods contained here. Of course, committed lands analysis may not suit a town's circumstances: there may be no underused capital facilities. However, the more general assumptions about contemporary planning on which the analysis is based undoubtedly apply in most towns. Committed lands analysis, simply summarized, is a method to make the goals of land use planning understandable and useful.

When first devising the method, the authors interviewed many leaders within the development community. During the course of these interviews, it quickly became clear that these individuals shared the primary concern of the authors: making clear the connection between the location of development and public service costs. The suggested reform was based on the common perception that every resident pays for public services through tax payments, and every resident wants them to be as low as possible. Interviewing these leaders was a start to making the idea of committed lands more salient in the development community, a beginning that was built on by periodic newletters describing the progress of the research.

The resulting chapters have offered a new way for planners and developers to support their ideas, rather than a new governmental structure. The book also encourages planners to imagine their own innovative methods—such as committed lands analysis—for getting the active interests in land development to work together before sites are chosen and projects are designed. The primary aim of these reforms should be to reunite planners and their considerations with the actual process of land use decision-making in American towns.

PRACTICAL ADVICE FOR LOCAL GOVERNMENT PLANNERS

We realize that many towns are not going to attempt reforms on the order of committed lands analysis, although they might want better land use decisions to be made. To help such towns, planners must counteract the forces that make their advice seem dismissible. Our view is that planners must come to terms with the simple fact of intimacy in small towns, which makes elected officials relentlessly subject to the judgment of their constituents. If planners can understand and accept this reality, they can turn it to their advantage.

Even though local elected officials take on the many highly visible ceremonial duties of cutting ribbons and dedicating parks, their days are, in fact, mostly spent managing the public's business—letting contracts, overseeing county departments, and drafting budgets. The rest of their time is spent serving their constituents' individual needs. On any given day, elected officials might be challenged to justify their vote on a mill-levy or might be told about potholes the street department has passed by. Never far from the mind of persons holding civic office is one overarching concern, and that is how constituents see their performance. This preoccupation is not misplaced, for official behavior is, in fact, subject to continual appraisal in small jurisdictions. Meetings are open, and decisions on local matters fill columns in the daily newspaper. Moreover, townspeople presume accessibility to their public officials. Small town elected officials are called at home, written to, talked about. Theirs is the most public of public service jobs, and their every action is home-town drama, the subject of speculation, opinion, and rumor.

These are the operative circumstances of small-town local government, where easy or popular decisions are rare. Land use choices especially cause resentment because controversies are framed as group against group and outcomes as one group over another. In defending decisions on these matters, elected officials have to hear complaints about the planning staff that offered them advice. It happens this way: a developer who has been denied a request for a zoning change will object to interpretations of zoning ordinance requirements and disparage the planners who made them, labeling the staff as antibusiness, overeducated and rigid bureaucrats who don't know the real-world pressures on a person trying to make an honest living. Facing this angry constituent—who probably is at a minimum an acquaintance—elected officials have a delicate and unenviable task. They must answer for their vote, which implies defending the planning department's counsel, yet they must do so without antagonizing the developer-constituent. For many officials in this position, an appealing strategy is to agree with the disparaging remarks about the planning staff, thereby deflecting some of the attention away from the fact that their vote concurred with the staff. That is, faced with complaints about the decisions they made, elected officials tend to avoid substantive discussion by joining in the criticism of the planning staff's style.

Planners, especially those in small towns, must accept a fundamental axiom of local government: land use decisions almost inevitably cause complaints, and persons holding elected office will respond to them. Therefore, a successful planner anticipates this need to respond. We see this involving two equally important tasks. First, the advice planners give elected officials must be clear, unbiased, and logical. Whether dealing with a controversial proposal to build a large shopping center or an uncontested request for a zoning variance, staff reports must be of consistently high quality because there is no matter so small that a sloppily reasoned preparation will suffice. The reports may not be read before a vote is taken because busy elected officials tend to base decisions on what transpires at public hearings. But staff reports must nonetheless be clear, interesting, and accessible in their argument to the ordinary citizen. The report's quality is critical because of its usefulness after a decision has been made. When land use decisions cause complaint, elected officials should be able to rely on the staff's report which makes a strong and convincing case for the particular decision.

Second, in discharging their duties, planners must attend to matters of style. This means, quite simply, that planners' acts will convince an observer that they are committed community residents and their training can help bring about an agreeable future. Planners are easily characterized as outsiders. They most often do not work where they grew up; they are typically younger and better educated than the politicians, officials, and private businessmen whom they see every day. If this distance between the planning office and the community is not closed, staff members will be perceived as meddlesome experts trying out their theories on a town. Planners know they need the support of elected officials when land use decisions are made, but they also need backing in the informal meetings officials have with disgruntled constituents. This support can be achieved if a developer vilifying the planning staff can be seen as venting frustration rather than genuinely pointing out the staff's shortcomings. There are actions which planners can take to gain elected officials' support, and some of these will be explained in the sections which follow. It must be emphasized that these recommendations presuppose good professional work. Our belief is that there's no lack of good planners and good planning innovations. There is, however, a lack of conduct which reinforces the merit of planners' advice in the eyes of elected officials faced with constituents' complaints.

In determining whether or not to take the side of the planning department, elected officials rely on their own experience with the staff and they listen to what developers and property owners tell them about their business dealings with planners. In addition, officials have an ear for what the larger public thinks about the staff. Planners, in an important sense, are on display with all these groups, and should be thoughtful of the impression they make.

Persuasive conduct begins with first impressions. Generally, most citizens visit the planning department when they want something they only vaguely understand, such as a zoning variance for a fence or a building permit for a garage. The person usually thinks that these are small matters, hardly worthy of bureaucratic notice. The citizen, then, reluctantly enters an office where people with special skills are at work, reviewing plats and looking at oddly configured zoning maps. To most people, planners appear to be guardians of inaccessible knowledge, experts whose reasoning processes are distant from the concerns of ordinary folks.

Simple acts can help overcome this formidable impression—such as having a person greet people as they enter the planning office. This does not mean hiring a new staff member. Rather, greeting can be a 2-hour or 4-hour rotating duty for staff members who happen to have a personable side. It is easy to achieve a genuine personal style precisely because small towns (we include those with no more than 75,000 people) have just such expectations of intimacy. Residents know or have an impression of each other, they talk about civic affairs with a sense of potency, and they share shop talk.

Planners must remember that their expertise, despite its legitimate claims for providing an agreeable future, can easily set the office apart from the community. They must remind themselves that what they know is not arcane. Almost everybody has some sense of planning and can cite firsthand many positive examples. Planners, therefore, should not let the fact that they *can* talk like an expert allow them *to* talk like one. They should communicate in everyday terms that are appreciated in the town's avenues and shopping districts.

Through simplicity planners can use their education to a distinct advantage. It is assumed that planners have read extensively about the tools of professional practice and have been trained to notice how land

and the constructed environment can affect the way people live their lives. What takes special effort is the joining of the advantages of education and experience into a fresh perspective on the town's future. Such planners will be more persuasive than those speaking in the dreary language of planning textbooks: "spatially related clusters of uses" or "environmental suitability analysis."

A fact of planning practice is that the same issues must be explained over and over to different people: why parking is necessary, why the city has imposed landscaping requirements, and so forth. To the extent the planner's explanation seems rehearsed, stale, or boring, he or she will seem more condescending than convincing. Such a complaint will be heard and believed by an elected official. Explanations that are fresh and to the point are essential both for the information conveyed and the reception it receives. These are the essential ingredients of support for planning.

However, the freshest and most direct explanation demonstrated with the liveliest example may not put a smile on the frowning face of a landowner who hoped to be forgiven parking requirements in his new mini-mall. Often the best a planner can hope for is that the person will say, after hearing an explanation, "Well, yes, I understand that. But I don't like it." And even then, planners will watch the landowner walk down to the mayor's office to complain about the staff's uncooperative behavior. If the citizen can say he feels he has been treated fairly, the official hearing his complaint is more likely to conclude that the landowner's perception is understandable but not objectively true.

Fairness, which is obviously linked to clear communication, is the single most essential quality of professional conduct. Planners must even be fair with individuals who try to evade the comprehensive plan or avoid land use ordinances. Such requirements must be uniformly enforced, and yet planners must not earn a reputation for being rigid. This is largely a matter of professional style. Successful planners can explain vividly how any legislated requirement serves some public purpose (or else they should suggest it be changed). They can also make the case, and support it with examples, that to allow someone not to fulfill a requirement gives that person an unfair economic advantage over the developers who *do* build to the community's standards. Elected officials will find in this planner's argument an inherently compelling logic, even when faced with complaining constituents.

Fairness also requires that planners avoid categorizing individuals. To create a directory of people who have dodged land use regulations and whose projects should be reviewed with skepticism is counterproductive to good planning practice in small towns. Equally alien to good practice is listing preferred individuals who seem consistently to have "good" projects. Every project must be reviewed with equal care and accorded the same respect. Happily, in small towns, virtue is *not* its own reward. Rather, through the informal webs of Rotary and Kiwanis Clubs, home-builders associations, and the like, the actions of a cooperative, helpful, and fair planning staff will get advertised quickly. Planners' consistent fairness can turn this intimate quality of small towns to their advantage.

Popular epithets often belittle a planning office as overly intellectual or antibusiness. If planners are patient, sooner or later an opportunity will come along for dramatizing their necessary and helpful functions. In Missoula, for example, detractors routinely proclaimed the planning office as being antibusiness. One day, while a staff member was waiting for her suitcase at the airport, she noticed a sign above the baggage carousel. The sign advertised the slogan of a real estate company and read "Keep Montana Beautiful: Shoot a Land Developer." Funny, she thought, but also odd in a town where the chamber of commerce "Red Coats"—men and women dressed in red blazers—enthusiastically welcomed any arriving flight with a prospective businessman aboard. She wrote a letter to the airport director suggesting that this sign—even if it exemplified contemporary western wit—sent a signal that could be interpreted as antibusiness to potential investors. The airport director concurred and took the sign down; the local paper reported the incident, and editorials and letters-to-the-editor were written on both sides of the issue; the sign went back up for the remaining term of its lease, and then was permanently removed. The point to the anecdote is not whether the sign expressed an antibusiness sentiment, but that the planning office, by having criticized the sign, had acted in a way its detractors found unusual. They could not, thereafter, so easily consider planners as antibusiness. The drama was undoubtedly more effective than all the speeches we had previously given to insist that planners recognize the fundamental importance of business.

Another way of dramatizing their crucial role in town is for planners to invigorate the land use decisionmaking process. Landowners could be encouraged to experiment with new ways of presenting their proposals; videotapes of the town's typical subdivisions might be used in conjunction with a drawing of the site where a new subdivision is proposed. Rather than discussing an abstract development, participants in the hearing could be looking at what the project would most likely look like. Public hearings might become productive working sessions; using mechanical aids, people opposed to new projects could try to design something more suitable.

Enlisting Public Sentiment for Planning

Planners often do not take sufficient advantage of the intimacy of small towns. They do not keep the office routinely visible, yet they expect to be taken seriously during a controversy. There are many opportunities for planners to dramatize how integral the office is to everyday community life. For example, the local newspaper in Missoula has an editorial policy to print every letter it receives. This policy allowed Missoula planners to comment on important issues, read responses from interested citizens, and prevent the planning department from appearing to be a vestigial part of government. When planners are asked to make luncheon speeches to local organizations, they should see these engagements not as walk-throughs but as opportunities to explain what the planning office does and how it looks at the community. Similarly, planners should actively join in community life. For example, Missoula's Chamber of Commerce initiated a series of seminars about civic affairs for beginning management personnel in Missoula. The planning office sent three of its younger staff members to this "Leadership Missoula" series, not only for them to learn information about how the town works, but to get them to socialize with people they did not ordinarily see.

The examples of community involvement given above might suggest that public interactions are all pleasant. They are not. One of the more uncomfortable parts of being a planner is listening to an opponent's characterization of the staff. However, as hard as it might be, the wise planner will not become defensive but will remain sincerely open to what is being said. Often what people say is right within some limited context; harsh criticism may contain a workable insight even if it is not conclusive. The point is that part of a planner's style—which is important in an elected official's overall evaluation of planning staff—is how the inevitable criticism or unpleasantness is received.

This negative environment suggests how important it is that the planning office be a comfort to the staff. Humor should be encouraged there, and staff meetings should underscore the commonness of problems and aims. Disagreements among staff members will be routine and should be aired inside, but the office must appear united to the public it serves and to elected officials. Dissension made public cannot be tolerated because the job of local government planning has enough detractors. Opponents' belief in bad planning motives should not be abetted by bickering staff members.

Fortifying Support from Elected Officials

The preceding sections recommended how planners should interact with the public, taking the view that planners must recognize that citizens are constituents of elected officials. Planners must also consider how to deal with the elected officials themselves—the people whose support is most directly related to good land use decisions.

When complaints about the planning staff become routine, politicians can easily believe that the alleged faults are true. At the very least, an elected official needs to be able to say in response that corrective action has been taken. For this reason, it is useful to reorganize periodically the position of the planning staff in government. Planning departments are often combined with the building inspection office, for example, so that a person need only go to one place to get everything necessary for a building permit. In terms of efficiency and ease of the customer, it is an organization that makes sense. However, such an arrangement can make the planning department seem the sole obstacle to developing land. The department could be reorganized—even if there never will be a single best way to stop all complaints—in response to the concerns of the community. Planners insist that their work is on behalf of the citizens' goals expressed in the comprehensive plan. By being willing to respond to citizens' complaints, planners solve an elected official's problem as well as act on their own claims that they serve worthwhile ideas for the good of the community.

Because of the nature of their duties (adhering to the adopted general plan and overseeing the realization of land use regulations), planners are frequently characterized as municipal scolds. To offset this reputation, planners should keep track of and remark on their good results; for example the little saplings that grow into pleasant shade trees, the corners where traffic moves easily, the playgrounds where kids are safe, and so on. Planners might also take notice of improvements that are pleasing, but that weren't required. The professional staff should compliment the town. They might make design awards each year to developers and business owners; or, more simply, write letters praising noteworthy land development efforts. The simple act of commenting on good deeds eludes many small town planners; they are thereby deprived of an opportunity to close the distance between themselves and the rest of the community. Planners, after all, are simply community members who have had the good fortune to study planning, and have, therefore, special skills and insights to contribute.

What we have written is an attempt to help planners persuade elected officials to take the staff's advice. But planners must also know when they've lost on an issue. As important as it is—both for the sake of professional pride and for gaining support from people inclined to take planning's side—that the staff "fight the good fight," it is equally important that planners not be seen as hidebound elitists who cannot see any logic but their own. Planners should not expect to win in every case. (Frankly, planning logic can't be that good.) Nor should planners fight to the death on every issue. This is not a defeatist attitude; opportunities recur and a well-argued point will get to be made again when more information is available and decisionmakers are more familiar with the terms of the argument. If planners can see themselves as integral parts of the community, they will know that their efforts will accumulate good results over time.

A planner's desire to be effective with elected officials can lead to concentration on the one or more county commissioners or city council members who already are persuaded by good land use planning. Many planners will rely on that person's support in votes and in cloakroom meetings. This singular reliance is a mistake because it ignores the political world of the elected officials and because it almost inevitably leads to planners' disappointment. Elected officials have a diverse constituency of voters with broad, rather than deep interests. On election day in small towns, an incumbent must appear to have worked for the many different voters who judge performance in terms of short-term issues rather than long-term betterment of the community. Elected leaders may be lauded on retirement for service to the broader community, even for their vision, but this is not ready currency in elections. While in office they cannot appear to favor one department. Constituents have to believe elected officials have based their votes on their constituents'— not a department's—welfare. Furthermore, the impulse to work most closely with a sympathetic official leads planners to avoid the officials who seem hostile. This, too, is a mistake because it makes planners seem dismissible and invites action against them. Planners must try to gain the support of all officials, even those most opposed to the regulatory and advisory functions of the planning staff.

The point to the preceding discussion is important enough to be repeated. Planners, by the quality of their professional work and by their manner in discharging their duties, must ever attempt to gain formal and informal support for their advice. Substance and style have to comple-ment one another, especially in small towns where the closeness of the community is a fact of consequence.

PRODUCTIVE LOCAL GOVERNMENT PLANNING

Planners remain outside actual decisionmaking processes not only because elected officials and developers choose to ignore them and the public does not seem to support them, but also because of their own feelings of frustration regarding the developments elected officials sanction. Possibly the central lesson of committed lands analysis is its underlying philosophy: to take things as they are and improve them. To rejoin the decisionmaking process, planners need to adopt a similar philosophy. Fresh from graduate programs, planners come to work for local governments full of hope. When their enthusiasm meets the obstacles of municipal logic and public opposition, planners frequently become cynics, describing themselves as philosopher kings without a kingdom or as modern-day Cassandras. These are the planners who abandon their original professional aspirations and take a disdainful attitude toward the way land use decisions get made. Often such planners, looking for something new to re-engage their enthusiasm, will express a wish to work for a more enlightened community, or in a state with more progressive legislation. The condition is radical disaffection:

> So far, I thought, I had hardly met anyone in America who was immersed in anything. One look was enough; then you turned to something else . . . The same with the villages, they were never immersed in the landscape, they were always plunked on top of it; they stood out from their surroundings and seemed to have been put there by accident.[2]

But planners are not philosopher kings, nor are they Cassandras. They are citizens of the town that employs them, and they have been hired to use their training to help that town realize a truly pleasant civic future. No small part of this, particularly in slowly growing towns, is to make existing conditions better. If planners choose to immerse themselves in things as they are, they will appreciate the qualities that uniquely describe a community. They know what a novelist describing St. Louis knows:

> But all cities are ideas, ultimately. They create themselves, and the rest of the world apprehends them or ignores them as it chooses.[3]

Planners work best who do not belittle what seems inefficient or even ugly in a town; they seek in these features what is redeeming, what is integral to the town's idea of itself, and work creatively to enhance those features. An observation of Henry James encapsulates this better attitude:

> The things that have lasted . . . "succeed" as no newness . . . succeeds, inasmuch as their success is a created interest. There we catch the golden truth . . . that production takes time, and that the production of interest, in particular, takes *most* time.[4]

This remark applies readily to the discussion here. It suggests that professional aspirations for rationality must be tempered with some regard for individual expression and idiosyncrasy if interest is to result and if a town is to succeed in James's use of the word. It suggests a new phrase for planners who discover and build upon interest in their town: productive planners. This book contends that productive planners will adopt the underlying philosophy of committed lands analysis and realize their job is to make the world better, not to make it over.

An example might help make clear this translation of the philosophy of committed lands analysis to the planners' view of their function in civic life. Consider a typical urban nemesis: the jumble of establishments, neon signs, and congested traffic of the strip commercial development leading out of town. Ask planners what to do with the strip in their town and you're likely to hear, "Bulldoze it and start over." In fact, if the strip were bulldozed, the same forces that caused its creation in the first place would inevitably resurface. Americans prize convenience in its every aspect—convenient parking, convenient shopping, convenient location—and these desires foster strip commercial development. Bulldoze it, and it would reappear. Furthermore, if it were agreed that the same shops could exist and the same amount of parking could be provided, who would design the strip? If one person or a committee of interested citizens were chosen, the result would be without variety and predictably dull because it would be created from one person's imagination or a narrow consensus. Variety of development may be the one pleasing attribute of the strip, and a planner is better employed imagining how to make that commercial district ever increasingly more pleasant than imagining how to negate the strip or what to do with the land if it were cleared.

Observations About What Americans Have Built

Shortly before he died, Bernard DeVoto gave the Maine coast a brisk going over in his *Harper's* column, using some four-letter words that raised the hackles of the inhabitants. Mr. DeVoto used the word "slum" and the word "neon." He said that the highway into Maine was a sorry mess all the way to Bucksport, and that the whole strip was overpopulated and full of drive-ins, diners, souvenir stands, purulent amusement parks, and cheap-Jack restaurants. I was thinking about this indictment at lunch the other day, trying to reconstruct my own cheap-Jack impressions of the familiar route over it . . .

. . . [T]he road into Maine does not seem a slum to me. Like highways everywhere, it is a mixed dish: Gulf and Shell, bay and gull, neon and sunset, cold comfort and warm, the fussy facade of a motor court right next door to the pure geometry of an early-nineteenth-century clapboard house with barn attached. You can certainly learn to spell "moccasin" while driving into Maine, and there is often little else to do, except steer and avoid death. Woods and fields encroach everywhere, creeping to within a few feet of the neon and the court, and the experienced traveler into this land is always conscious that just behind the garish roadside stand, in its thicket of birch and spruce, stands the delicate and well-proportioned deer; just beyond the overnight cabin, in the pasture of granite and juniper, trots the perfectly designed fox. This is still our triumphant architecture, and the Maine man does not have to penetrate in depth to be excited by his coastal run; its flavor steals into his consciousness with the first ragged glimpse of properly textured woodland, the first whiff of punctually drained cove.[5]

E. B. White

Productive planners take heart from small successes, recognizing that well-planned communities are the result of individual decisions. These planners will not denigrate the importance of getting sidewalks installed in a subdivision because they recognize that planning goals are written in terms of abstract community interests, but that individuals and families find happiness going about their daily lives unimpeded. While good planning might be invisible to nonplanners, it isn't to productive planners who make it their business to realize over and over again the smallest instances of good planning. Productive planners can use these examples as ways to explain plainly how planning can bring about community benefit. Productive planners know that there are all manner of bad land use decisions that need to be corrected or avoided in the future, but they seek only to correct the worst problem in their community as a start. Later, they work on other problems.

Finally, productive planners read a literature broader than their profession's journals. This book has contained several "Observations About What Americans Have Built" to bring to its readers the thoughts of articulate laymen regarding the world that results from local land use decisions. Accordingly, a concluding counsel for productive planning comes from contemporary fiction. (When reading it, local place names may be substituted for "New Jersey.")

> Though I am not displeased by New Jersey. Far from it. Vice implies virtue to me, even in landscape, and virtue value. An American would be crazy to reject such a place, since it is the most diverting and readable of landscapes, and the language is always American.
> Better to come to earth in New Jersey than not to come at all. Or worse, to come to your senses in some spectral place like Colorado or California, or to remain up in the dubious airs searching for some right place that never existed and never will. Stop searching. Face the earth wherever you can. Literally speaking, it's all you have to go on. Indeed, in its homeliest precincts and turnouts, the state feels as unpretentious as Cape Cod once might've, and its bustling suburban-with-good-neighbor-industry mix of life makes it the quintessence of the town-and-country spirit. Illusion will never be your adversary here.[6]

Illusion for many planners is their drive to make the world wholly efficient, logical, and rational. This attitude *is* an adversary to productive planning. It misses the unique qualities and idiosyncratic ideas that can provide interest and diversion to people living in a town. It seeks a "better" world that probably does not exist and never can. This book has presented a method and argued for an attitude toward American towns that could be productive because they are grounded in the practical realities of what actually exists. Committed lands analysis accepts past mistakes and tries to ameliorate their ongoing consequences; the book's philosophy in its analysis of local towns is generous and not condemning. Although most of the mistakes that committed lands analysis responds to are the clear result of local choice, the book recognizes that citizen preference also contributes to the sense of vitality that any town must have if it is to succeed as a place where residents can find lives of well-being.

NOTES

1. Montana Codes Annotated, 76-1-102(1).

2. Peter Handke, "Short Letter, Long Farewell," in *3 × Handke* (New York: Collier Books, Macmillan Publishing Company, 1988).

3. Jonathan Franzen, *The Twenty-Seventh City* (New York: Farrar, Straus, and Giroux, 1988) p. 13.

4. Henry James, *The American Scene* (Bloomington: Indiana University Press, 1968).

5. E. B. White, *Essays of E.B. White* (New York: Harper and Row, 1977), pp 8–9.

6. Richard Ford, *The Sportswriter* (New York: Vintage Contemporaries, 1986), pp. 52–53.

APPENDIX A

CALCULATION APPENDIX

The committed lands analytic method calculates the net gain in efficiency that is the result of serving new customers from an existing public facility. Chapter 4 presented the calculations necessary for a wastewater treatment plant. The pages that follow offer a step-by-step description of how changes to production and distribution efficiency can be measured for three other types of major capital facilities: public schools, water supply systems, and fire protection assets. These four types of facilities were chosen because each of their attributes are different, and when taken together include every type of public service offered by local jurisdictions. That is, these are meant to be examples of how committed lands analysis can guide your thinking not only about the public assets discussed in Chapter 4 and this appendix, but about other major capital facilities in which your municipality has invested.

You will find in the pages which follow many examples of the process of adapting existing data to the purposes of committed lands analysis. Because this analysis is new, decisions made by local governments regarding how to keep records may not conform with the data requirements of this method. For that reason, the appendix will use proxy measures for individual pieces of information—proxy measures that your municipality may not have. We recommend that in consultation with local officials, you begin seeking measures that correspond to those used in our case study examples. If you tailor the committed lands analysis to your community's recordkeeping standards, it will enhance your working relationship with the knowledgeable administrators of public facilities and make the process of guiding growth more likely to be commonly accepted. We offer only one admonition: whatever measures you choose must have a consistent mathematical and fiscal basis.

The description of how to calculate efficiency for each of three major public assets follows the order that appeared in Chapter 4 for a wastewater treatment facility. The appendix will discuss the items listed below:

The results of these calculations would be entered on the Committed Lands Summary Sheet, explained in Chapter 4, pages 87–88.

PUBLIC WATER SUPPLY

This section is designed to provide a guide to your assessment of the water distribution system currently in place in your community, using committed lands analysis. The method developed here allows you to estimate the gains in efficiency brought by new customers connecting to an existing public water supply that has excess capacity.

Relevant Characteristics

The provision of water to new residential and commercial development can be accomplished through a variety of different methods. These methods can be conveniently divided into two categories: private wells and public water systems. Committed lands analysis will determine the net benefit to the community from new customers being added to the public water system and also ascribe a cost to the community from a new project being allowed to drill a private well. The costs are based on the lost opportunity to increase production efficiency, although there are other, here unquantified, costs of private wells.

Private wells may be drilled and installed at little public expense, although private wells may draw down the water table and reduce artesian pressure in the aquafer used by the public water supply. While this external effect of private wells is well recognized, there is no generally accepted method for estimating cost. Furthermore, private wells generally do not have capacity to provide fire protection unless large storage reservoirs (containing at least 3,000 gallons) are provided, or unless adequate sprinkler systems are installed in new buildings. Because most private residences do not have such firefighting facilities, by choosing to drill their own wells they, in fact, increase the fire danger to other homes and empty lands nearby. In this case also, there is no generally accepted method for estimating the public cost. Therefore, although the committed lands method recognizes the significance of these wider consequences, only opportunity cost will be used to measure the fiscal effects of private decisions to drill wells. That opportunity cost represents the lost chance to increase production efficiency in a public water supply system that has available excess capacity.

Analysis of Efficiency

To calculate the net gain in efficiency brought by new customers, five determinations must be made:

1. Common basis for defining a customer of the facility;

2. Capacity and current utilization of the facility, expressed in terms of standard customers;

3. Yearly fixed obligation for the facility;

4. Change in production efficiency caused by new customers; and

5. Delivery costs that are related to the location of a customer.

The following text shows you how to make these determinations in order to estimate your community's net gain from adding new customers to its public water system.

Definition of Customers. As explained in Chapter 4, the number of customers is expressed in terms of standard customers. For the case of public water supplies, the amount of water used by a customer is associated with the size of the water meter. The average single-family dwelling unit uses 5/8-inch or 3/4-inch disc meters, capable of delivering 400 gallons per day—the typical volume of water used in Montana by a single-family house.[1] We will use this as the measure of a standard customer. Using the table that follows, the committed lands analyst can determine the demand for water that any particular land use will generate in terms of standard customers.

Capacity and Current Utilization. With the definition of customer provided, you can define the capacity and current utilization of the public water system in terms of standard customers.

- Measure engineering capacity of the plant in gallons available per day. The figure would be divided by 400 to determine the number of standard customers.
- Measure current use of the facility in gallons pumped per day. Again,

Table 1

Description	Standard Customers
Meter size: ⅝ or ¾ inches (The typical meter used in single family dwellings):	1.00
Other meter sizes:	
1 inch:	2.0
1-¼ inches:	3.0
1-½ inches:	4.0
2 inches:	6.4
3 inches:	12.0
4 inches:	20.0
6 inches:	40.0
8 inches:	64.0

divide that figure by 400 to determine the number of standard customers currently provided water.

Calculate the available unused capacity by subtracting the existing standard customers from the number of standard customers the plant is capable of processing.

If you determine that your system is within 10 percent of capacity,[2] the required analysis is outside the scope of the committed lands method. In this case you should determine the costs of system expansion in consultation with the city engineer and refer to the section of Chapter 4 entitled "Investment Decisions for Assets Nearing Full Capacity," (page 91) for additional guidance.

Yearly Fixed Obligation for the Public Water System.   As explained in Chapter 4, we will use yearly fixed obligations as the basis for measuring gains in production efficiency for the water system. These obligations include the costs for the current year's operations, maintenance, depreciation, replacement, and debt service; these costs are paid by the bills sent to the system's users. To determine the total obligation, acquire a copy of the current budget for the public water system and sum the expenditures for the items just listed. The total amount should be reduced by any federal or state subsidies for particular items and should also be reduced by any revenue gained by selling water to customers outside the community.

Efficient Production of Services.   If there is excess capacity, you can determine the gain in production efficiency brought by a new customer's hooking up to the existing water supply system. The formula for calculating change in production efficiency appears below:

$$\left\{ \frac{\text{Yearly Fixed Obligation}}{\substack{\text{Current Standard}\\\text{Customers}}} - \frac{\text{Yearly Fixed Obligation}}{\substack{\text{Current Standard}\\\text{Customers} + 1}} \right\} \times \substack{\text{Number of}\\\text{Current Standard}\\\text{Customers}}$$

This formula is readily understood. The addition of one standard customer will lower the average fixed cost of service to all existing users and leave the variable cost of service unchanged. This means that each user—new and old—will share the burden of the cost of supplying potable water. As long as there is excess capacity, committed lands analysis equates gains in production efficiency with the cost reductions that occur because costs are shared.

Efficient Distribution of Services.   The distribution of services for a water system involves connection with a water main which delivers the required flow for daily water needs. While several research studies have both proven that delivery costs for water rise with distance from the customer and have shown how these costs might be estimated, the analysis is more complicated than is practical for communities of the size for which committed lands analysis is intended.[3] Although the importance of such analysis cannot be ignored, its sophistication is unnecessary for relatively small, slow-growing communities. If in the future a simple measure is devised which can easily impute costs to distance, we will rewrite this section of the appendix. At this point we will simply assume that water is efficiently distributed to persons who connect to the supply, and that the marginal cost of different locations is zero.

Calculation: Net Gain in Efficiency

Calculating net gain in efficiency is simple. Since there is no cost of distribution related to location, the net gain in efficiency is simply the figure you calculate for change in production efficiency. This figure, you will recall, is the gain brought by each additional standard customer. If a proposed project were to encompass, say, ten standard customers, the net gain in efficiency would be the change in production efficiency multiplied by ten.[4]

Case Study

This case study will illustrate how to calculate changes in efficiency resulting from new customers hooking up to the community's water system. The data comes from Missoula, Montana, and is representative of the experience of towns for which committed lands analysis was designed.

    1. The first step in this case study is to gather the data necessary for the analysis:

        a. Capacity and Current Utilization

        Current total volume of water being supplied in Missoula is the equivalent of 30,000 standard customers; this is less than 50 percent of available water supply. There is adequate supply for almost any project likely to occur under the growth rates projected for the city and county during the next 5 to 10 years.

        b. Yearly Fixed Obligations for the Water System

        $4,057,976 - This figure represents the annual budget for the water system and does not include any revenue gained from federal or state sources, or from selling water outside Missoula.[5]

    2. The second step is to calculate the change in production efficiency. Simply insert the appropriate information into the formula presented above:

$$\frac{\$4,057,976}{30,000} - \frac{\$4,057,976}{30,001} \times 30,000$$

$$= (\$135.2659 - \$135.2614) \times 30,000$$
$$= \$.0045 \times 30,000 = \$135.00$$

This means that adding one standard customer to the system saves $.0045 per existing customer, and that the total gain in efficiency for the community is $135.

    3. Discussion

This measure of $135 system savings is the base measure of efficiency gain used for comparison in committed lands analysis. First, it is the practical measure of committed lands: if the new customer located where no new mains must be extended, the community will realize the total increase in efficiency of $135. At any other location, the net gain in efficiency will have to be reduced by the costs of extending services, as discussed in Chapter 4 under the heading "Prudent Expansion of Committed Lands." This fact allows comparisons to be made among different potential locations for development.

Second, this base measure allows us to quantify the cost of allowing new customers to drill their own wells. Without increasing variable costs, each potential customer could have saved the community a total of $135 in fixed cost burden. The committed lands analyst will consider this the opportunity cost to the community of not inducing a customer to connect to the public water supply. And finally, the $135 figure sets the upper limit on the value of inducements given to the potential user to connect to the system.

FIRE PROTECTION

The following section provides a guide to using committed lands analysis to assess the fire protection services currently in place in your community. The method developed here allows you to estimate the gains in efficiency brought by new customers locating within a fire district with excess capacity.

Relevant Characteristics

Fire protection is provided under a rating system developed by the Insurance Service Office (ISO). The rating system measures the ability of the fire department to respond to normally occurring demands for service, and is used to set private insurance rates within jurisdictional boundaries. This means that the level of service can be quantified and chosen as a matter of public policy. For the purposes of committed lands analysis we will assume that the level of service as measured by the ISO rating will not change as a result of the location of new users within a fire protection service area.

Analysis of Efficiency

To calculate the net gain in efficiency brought by new customers, five determinations must be made:

    1. Common basis for defining a customer of the facility;

2. Capacity and current utilization of the facility, expressed in terms of standard customers;

3. Yearly fixed obligation for the facility;

4. Change in production efficiency caused by new customers; and

5. Delivery costs that are related to the location of a customer.

The following text will show you how to make these determinations in order to estimate your community's net gain from adding new customers to fire protection districts.

Definition of Customers.   Relying on ISO standards, committed lands analysis will consider all households and commercial enterprises equivalent fire risks, unless they have a special risk designation by the ISO. If a particular project has such a special risk designation, you should consult with the rural or city fire chief to determine a measure of demand for fire protection as a multiple of the demand associated with a single structure. A standard customer, then, is a structure.

Capacity and Current Utilization.   In consultation with the fire chief, the analyst will determine whether there is sufficient capacity in the current fire protection facilities to accommodate any proposed new use. This measure is somewhat different from that suggested for other capital facilities, but it is appropriate to the nature of fire protection.

If you determine that your fire protection facilities are within 10 percent of capacity, or if adding new users will cause the ISO rating to change, the required analysis is outside the scope of the committed lands methodology. In this case you should determine (in consultation with the rural or city fire chief) the costs of system expansion and refer to the section of Chapter 4 entitled "Investment Decisions for Assets Nearing Full Capacity," (page 91) for additional guidance.

Yearly Fixed Obligations for Fire Protection.   As explained in Chapter 4, we will use yearly fixed obligations as the basis for measuring gains in production efficiency for fire protection services. These obligations include the costs for the current year's operations, maintenance, depreciation, replacement, and debt service; these are costs paid out of taxes levied on customers served by fire protection districts. To arrive at this figure, simply use the budget for the particular fire district where a project would be located and total the expenditures necessary for the items just listed. From this sum you should deduct any subsidies from federal and state sources.

Efficient production of services.   If there is excess capacity, you can determine the gain in production efficiency brought by a new customer's moving within an existing fire protection district. The formula for calculating change in production efficiency appears below:

$$\left\{ \frac{\text{Yearly Fixed Obligation}}{\substack{\text{Current Standard} \\ \text{Customers}}} - \frac{\text{Yearly Fixed Obligation}}{\substack{\text{Current Standard} \\ \text{Customers} + 1}} \right\} \times \substack{\text{Number of} \\ \text{Current Standard} \\ \text{Customers}}$$

This formula is readily understood. The addition of one standard customer will lower the average fixed cost of service to all existing users and leave the variable cost of service unchanged. This means that each user—new and old—will share the burden of the cost of fire protection. As long as there is excess capacity, committed lands analysis equates gains in production efficiency with the cost reductions that occur because costs are shared.

Efficient distribution of services.   Firefighting services must be available to users on demand, although they will be used only sporadically. Compared to the cost of keeping the firefighting services in a constant state of readiness, the cost of responding to an emergency alarm is negligible. Therefore, we will not include a cost of distribution for such services.

Calculation: Net Gain in Efficiency

The calculation is simple: since there is no cost of distribution related to location, the net gain in efficiency is simply the figure you calculate for change in production efficiency. This figure, you will recall, is the gain brought by each additional standard customer. If a proposed project were to encompass, say, ten standard customers, the net gain in efficiency would be the change in production efficiency multiplied by ten.[6]

Case Study

This case study will illustrate how to calculate changes in efficiency resulting from new customers locating within a fire protection district with excess capacity. The data comes from Missoula, Montana, and is representative of the experience of towns for which committed lands analysis was designed.

   1. The first step in this case study is to gather the data necessary for the analysis:

   a. Number of Existing Customers

As explained earlier, each structure is considered a standard customer. Although we don't have an accurate count of such structures, we do have the number of tax bills sent in each fire district. Until such time as an actual count can be made, we suggest using the number of tax bills as the proxy measure for the number of structures. We realize this will understate the current number of customers when one considers large industrial complexes under a single ownership. However, such complexes (at least in Missoula) have their own fire protection departments and hence will in fact make fewer demands on the public service than other, smaller customers.

The total number of tax bills in the City of Missoula is 10,446. This is the measure of the number of existing standard customers.

   b. Capacity and Current Utilization

Assume the fire chief has said there is adequate capacity for the project being considered.

   c. Yearly Fixed Obligations for Fire Protection

$1,955,199 - This figure represents the annual budget for fire protection services in the city, and is exclusive of any revenue gained from federal or state sources.[7]

   2. The second step is to calculate the change in production efficiency. Simply insert the appropriate information into the formula presented above:

$$\frac{\$1,955,199}{10,446} - \frac{\$1,955,199}{10,447} \times 10,446$$
$$= (\$187.1720 - 187.1541) \times 10,446$$
$$= .0179 \times 10,446 = \$186.98$$

This means that adding one standard customer to the district saves $.0179 per existing customer, and that the total gain in efficiency for the district is $186.98.

   3. Discussion

The measure of $186.98 savings is the base measure of efficiency gain used for comparison in committed lands analysis. First, it is the practical measure of committed lands: if the new customer located where existing fire protection facilities could accommodate the structure, the persons living in the particular fire district would realize the total increase of $186.98. Second, it allows comparisons among different fire protection districts in terms of the benefits to be gained by locating within them.

PUBLIC SCHOOLS

This section provides a guide to using committed lands analysis to your assessment of the public schools currently in place in your community. The method developed here allows you to estimate the gains in efficiency brought by new customers using an existing system of public schools.

Relevant Characteristics

Public schools provide education for young people in communities, although the benefits of education are commonly believed to be enjoyed by all residents, not just the students who attend school. The cost of public education is typically associated with location through the administrative device of local school districts. The district manages the educational facilities and is responsible for the budget. The locally raised portion of that budget is generated through mill levies on property located within the district.

The following discussion recognizes the difficult issues of equity inherent in financing schools based on the value of property located within individual school districts. However, the goal of committed lands analysis is to make existing investments pay off under present circumstances, by which we mean the constitutional and statutory directives for public school finance as currently codified. If future legislation or judicial decisions change the statutes which specify how public education is to be paid for, we will rewrite this section accordingly.

Analysis of Efficiency

To calculate the net gain in efficiency brought by new customers, five determinations must be made:

1. Common basis for defining a customer of the facility;
2. Capacity and current utilization of the facility, expressed in terms of standard customers;
3. Yearly fixed obligation for the facility;
4. Change in production efficiency caused by new customers; and

5. Delivery costs that are related to the location of a customer.
The following text shows you how to make these determinations in order
to estimate your community's net gain from adding new customers to its
public school system.

Definition of Customers.   You will recall that the definition of standard
customers made it possible for a committed lands analyst to measure the
gains in efficiency brought by new customers. For wastewater treatment
plants and the public water supply, you could compare different types of
land uses in terms of "how much" water they needed, or how much
sewage they produced. Public schools require a slightly different measure of customer for the reason that the benefits of public education are
generally taken to fall on all residents rather than on only the students
attending school.

The current budget for any school year reflects the commitment made
by the school district in its existing facilities, staff, and the number of
students being served. Based on the results of popular elections to raise
additional revenue, the school board may make changes to the curricu-
lum, to extracurricular activities, and to the physical facilities. We will
define the consumer of education services as a household. Households
represent consumers of the public education service, consumers whose
decisions in school district elections determine the level of locally
generated revenues in their particular school districts.

The measure of standard customers for public schools, therefore, will
be households. Remember that this is the number to be used in the
calculation of gains in efficiency. For commercial and industrial projects,
the value to the community of particular locations is understood by
traditional economic arguments that the development will add to the
assessed valuation in the school district without adding to the demand
for public education. Because we have defined gains in efficiency in
terms of yearly fixed obligations, the change in assessed valuation will
not directly affect efficiency in the production of education. Rather, the
effect will be felt in future years, and for this reason we consider it
indirect and recommend that commercial and industrial projects not be
evaluated for efficiency gains in public education.

Capacity and Current Utilization.   For purposes of this discussion, we
will define capacity and current utilization as follows:
   • Capacity of the schools, by school district, in terms of available
     classroom space; and

• Enrollment in the schools, by school district.

Simple subtraction of current enrollment from current capacity will yield the available capacity for new students. If you determine that the available classroom space is within 10 percent of capacity,[8] the required analysis is outside the scope of committed lands methodology. In this case you should determine the costs of providing more space—by building more classrooms, or by going on double shifts, to name two obvious alternatives—in consultation with the school board, and refer to the section of Chapter 4 entitled "Investment Decisions for Assets Nearing Full Capacity," (page 91) for additional guidance.

Yearly Fixed Obligations for Public Schools. As explained in Chapter 4, we will use yearly fixed obligations as the basis for measuring gains in production efficiency for public schools. These obligations include the costs for the current year's operations, maintenance, depreciation, replacement, and debt service; these are costs paid out of current taxes levied on residents of the school district. To find out the total obligation, simply acquire the school district's annual budget and total the expenditures necessary for the items just listed. Deduct from this figure any subsidies from federal and state sources, including any revenues received under state equalization formulas. You should also deduct any fees received from individual users for special services.

Efficient Production of Services. If there is excess capacity, you can determine the gain in production efficiency brought by a new customer's moving within an existing school district. The formula for calculating change in production efficiency appears below:

$$\left\{ \frac{\text{Yearly Fixed Obligation}}{\text{Current Standard Customers}} - \frac{\text{Yearly Fixed Obligation}}{\text{Current Standard Customers} + 1} \right\} \times \frac{\text{Number of Current Standard Customers}}{}$$

This formula is readily understood. The addition of one standard customer will lower the average fixed cost of service to all existing users. This means that each user—new and old—will share the burden of the cost of public education. As long as there is excess capacity, committed lands analysis equates gains in production efficiency with the cost reductions that occur because costs are shared.

Efficient Delivery of Services. Delivery costs are simply determined: Montana requires busing for children living at least three miles from school, but as a practical matter school districts elect to pick up children who live closer. Committed lands analysis recognizes three different situations which may occur with regard to location of new residential uses:

1. No additional costs of busing:
   - If a new residential project is located within the generally accepted walking distance of the school, there is no additional cost related to location of new students.
   - If a new residential project is located on an existing bus route with available space for additional students, there is no additional cost related to location.
2. Additional costs of busing:

If a new residential project is located where a bus route will have to be extended, we recommend using the annual district-wide per mile cost of busing, multiplied by the number of miles added onto the route, to determine the new costs of transporting children to school. The formula below describes the calculation:

(Average yearly cost of busing per mile × Additional miles traveled)

3. Additional costs of parents' driving children:

Where there is no bus service, school districts pay parents a statutorily defined rate per mile if they live farther than three miles from the school. In such cases, the cost of distribution is the distance multiplied by the rate for each day in a school year. The formula is as follows:

(Households × Statutory daily rate) × days in attendance

Calculation: Net Gain in Efficiency

The calculation is simple: you subtract from the gain in production efficiency any additional costs incurred for transporting new students to a school with excess capacity. The result represents the net gain in efficiency for a school district brought by each additional standard customer. If a proposed project were to encompass, say, ten standard customers, the net gain in efficiency would be the net gain multiplied by ten.[9]

Case Study

This case study shows you how to calculate changes in efficiency resulting from new customers locating within a school district with excess capacity. The data comes from Missoula, Montana, and is representative of the experience of towns for which committed lands analysis was designed.

1. The first step in this case study is to gather the data necessary for the analysis:

   a. Number of Existing Customers

   As explained earlier, each household is considered a standard customer. Although we don't have an accurate count of households in each school district, we have developed a proxy measure in consultation with school district administrators. The best approximation of households is the number of residential property tax bills issued within the school district. Until such time as an actual count of households is available by school district, we suggest using this proxy for standard customers. This information is usually available from the county assessor's office.

   The total number of residential tax bills issued in School District 1 is 18,921. This is the measure of the number of existing standard customers.

   b. Capacity and Current Utilization

   It should be noted that the capacity of schools is not expressed in standard customers. Rather, you would be interested in how many students a new residential project is likely to bring. We recommend using the figure calculated by the U.S. Census for Montana—0.6 children per household. That is, in determining whether a school has adequate classroom space for children likely to move into a subdivision of 50 houses, you would ask whether the building could hold 30 more children (50 houses × 0.6).

   School District 1 has adequate classroom space for approximately 750 more children.[10] For this example, we will assume that the proposed residential project will bring a small number of additional children, i.e., that there will be classroom space for them. We will also assume that the project is located on a school bus route that has ample seats for the additional children.

   c. Yearly Fixed Obligations for Public Education

   $5,654,176 - This figure represents the annual budget for School District 1, and does not include special fees received, nor any revenue gained from federal or state sources. That is, this is the total raised from local mill levies in the district.

2. The second step is to calculate the change in production efficiency.

You simply insert the appropriate information into the formula presented above:

$$\frac{\$5,654,176}{18,921} - \frac{\$5,654,176}{18,922} \times 18,921$$

$$= (\$298.8307 - \$298.8149) \times 18,921$$

$$= \$.0158 \times 18,921 = \$298.95$$

This means that adding one standard customer to the district saves $.0158 per existing customer, and that the total gain in efficiency for the school district is $298.95.

3. Discussion

The measure of $298.95 savings is the base measure of efficiency gain used for comparison in committed lands analysis. First, it is the practical measure of committed lands: if the new customer located where existing public schools could accommodate additional students, the persons living in the particular school district would realize the total increase of $298.95. Second, it allows comparisons among different school districts in terms of the benefits to be gained by locating within them.

NOTES

1. Brown and Caldwell, "Feasibility of Implementing Annexation Fees and Utility Development Charges." This report is available from Brown and Caldwell, Consulting Engineers; 28 Annette Park Drive; Bozeman, Montana 59715.

2. We suggest that when a public facility is operating within 10 percent of its capacity, there is ample time for your community to engage in planning to add to that capacity.

3. See for example, Robert M. Clark and Richard G. Stevie, "A Water Supply Cost Model Incorporating Spatial Variables," *Land Economics* **57** (February 1981): 558–66, for a discussion of the regression analysis necessary.

4. This is an approximation for small changes in the number of customers, and it is recommended so that the analysis need only be done once a year. However, if a proposed project would bring a large number of new customers, the analysis should be made by using Formula 1 (shown on page 79) with the actual number of new customers, rather than simply multiplying the per customer change by the number of new customers.

5. Missoula gets its water from a private company. We have used their budget as if it were a public water system—not an unacceptable proxy, since the city is now trying to purchase the system.

6. This is an approximation for small changes in the number of customers, and is recommended so that the analysis need only be done once a year. However, if a proposed project would bring a large number of new customers, the analysis should be made by using Formula 1 (shown on page 79) with the actual number of new customers, rather than simply multiplying the per customer change by the number of new customers.

7. The city maintains an ISO rating of 4.

8. We suggest that when a public facility is operating within 10 percent of its capacity, there is ample time for your community to engage in planning to add to that capacity.

9. This is an approximation for small changes in the number of customers, and it is recommended so that the analysis need only be done once a year. However, if a proposed project would bring a large number of new customers, the analysis should be made by using Formula 1 (shown on page 79) with the actual number of new customers, rather than simply multiplying the per customer change by the number of new customers.

10. Some individual schools are crowded in the district, but the taxpayers have chosen to bus children within the district to take advantage of excess capacity. We assume they will continue to do so.

APPENDIX B

SURVEY OF THE DEVELOPMENT COMMUNITY

In the early stages of the Committed Lands Research Project, we interviewed a structured sample of the people whom we hope will come to use the results of the research—the public and private participants in development decisions. There were 37 respondents, including realtors and land developers, bankers, accountants, appraisers, attorneys, insurors, surveyors, and leaders of business organizations. The purpose of the survey was to determine what information or analyses, if any, these decisionmakers might need from a growth guidance system, analyses and information now neglected by existing theory and practice. In addition, the survey measured the respondents' understanding of the relationship between development decisions and governmental costs as a way of determining what preliminary information must be included when the results of this research are explained to potential users. The responses to that survey are the subject of this appendix.

1. *Do you agree that the choice of a location for a development project could have an effect on public service costs?*

All but one of those surveyed agreed that location could affect public service costs. One business executive who has held public office is so convinced of the connection between location and taxpayer costs that he said, "There ought to be a different way to tax so as to force infill. The marginal increases in public service costs should be paid for by the person causing the increases."

Several persons noted that the amount of public service costs associated with a development could be lowered if some facilities were provided by the owners themselves, as, for example, when subdivisions have their own water supply or when houses are served by individual septic systems.

The single interviewee who disagreed believed that a development project could produce enough taxes to cover the costs it creates, no matter its location.

2. *In your opinion, what are the most important factors in choosing a site for a particular development?*

The following graphs show the most frequently mentioned factors and the percentage of respondents who cited those factors.

Note: **Available services** included primary and secondary education, public safety (fire and police protection), public works (roadways,

Factors for Choosing Residential Sites:

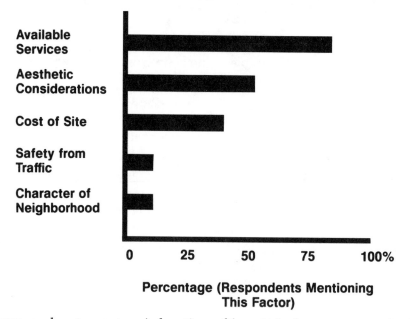

**Percentage (Respondents Mentioning
This Factor)**

sewers, and water systems), location of hospitals for emergency health care, and public transportation.

In addition to the factors shown above, a few people said convenience of shopping was important, as was the air quality of an area.

One developer noted that any factor would vary in importance according to the income of prospective buyers. For example, for people of limited means, the availability of public transportation might seem quite important—although the cost of the site would outweigh everything else; for people of more ample means, aesthetic considerations might rank highest, in part because other deficiencies can be overcome simply by paying to have them corrected.

One man who's built many houses throughout the state mentioned an idiosyncrasy of Montanans: "It doesn't matter if a person lives in a doublewide or a 4,000 square-foot custom home, people in Montana who live outside of town don't want to see their neighbors—or they don't want to see any more of them than they did the day they moved in."

Note: **Available services** meant public works and utilities; **location to market** meant how easily the site could be found by the customers a commercial concern hoped to attract; and **type of business** was a catch-all category whose definition simply suggested that different

Factors for Choosing Commercial Sites

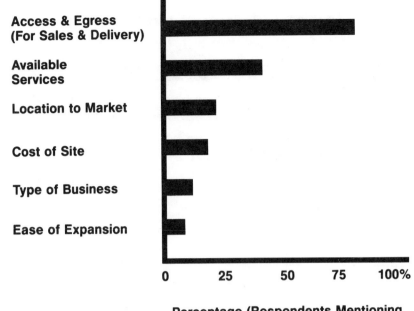

Percentage (Respondents Mentioning This Factor)

enterprises had different locational needs. For example, some firms profit by being near their competitors, some by being distant; some companies can only prosper if they can capture a "drive-by" clientele, while for others this factor is neglible.

One person cautioned that, "Like it or not, our society relies on strip development for convenience. For the businesses that get customers as they drive by, it's a terrible detriment **not** to face the highway. There's no way to avoid that type of development."

On the subject of customers' convenience, a business leader remarked that "We need an articulated, accepted, and reliable standard for neighborhood commercial shops."

The locational factors important to industrial concerns differ principally from commercial enterprises by reason of industry's sometimes making extraordinary demands on public services: special wastewater treatment facilities might be necessary, or roadways might have to be improved to accommodate frequent heavy truck traffic. Manufacturing sometimes requires unusual sites, such as places where unpleasant production processes, such as repellent smells or irritating noise, can be buffered from neighbors.

Several of the respondents remarked on the fact that Missoula has three commodious and well-serviced industrial parks, each with many

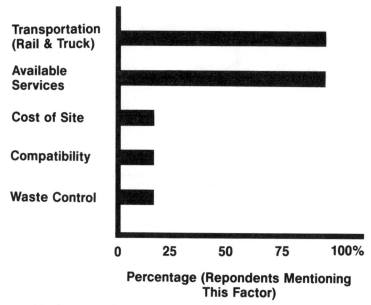

Factors for Choosing Industrial Sites

Transportation (Rail & Truck)

Available Services

Cost of Site

Compatibility

Waste Control

0   25   50   75   100%

Percentage (Repondents Mentioning This Factor)

vacancies. To their mind, this represents a significant waste of opportunity, as well as a costly fact of life here: we allow industrial uses to go "pretty much where they want," irrespective of the public investment already made to make particular areas especially suitable for manufacturing.

Additional Remarks Pertinent to all Types of Development

One business leader summarized all the information reported here with a simple sentence: "All factors can be reduced to profit." Indeed, the factors mentioned were attempts to specify what made a development—residential, commercial, or industrial—attractive enough to sell.

"People do things by circumstance, not logically," a realtor said, and several respondents inadvertently explained this remark by saying that people who decide to undertake some enterprise typically own a parcel of land already, and they will simply use that land without making an analysis of market factors. They can prosper, of course, and many do. But several respondents listed the failed business concerns and partially developed subdivisions that have followed from such uninformed locational decisions. And they mentioned delinquent SIDs as the price the public had to pay for failures of the private development sector.

Finally, several people mentioned the fact that decisions by governing bodies over whether to allow or deny projects of any sort were often unpredictable. This, they said, made the already risky business of development even more uncertain. A few respondents remarked that neither the comprehensive plan nor adopted zoning districts are reliable guides to what will get approved, and that this single fact causes developers to look for unzoned land beyond the jurisdiction of local land use controls that they believe are wielded capriciously.

3. *We envision developing a prototypical map to show vacant and usable land within existing service districts. Our idea is that proposed developments on these sites would have an easier time gaining public support and official approval. Would you use such a map in deciding where to site a new project? And if you would, what other information would you like to see included in such a map of committed lands?*

There was a positive response of 80 percent of the respondents who said the map **would** be useful and thought it should include the following:

- More specific information about the tracts themselves, including zoning and signage restrictions, land value, size, access, taxes, insurance rates, and the name of the landowner.
- Information which would give a sense of the communal context in which the vacant tract lies, such as its relationship to shopping and work sites, traffic patterns, difficulty in getting to the site during winter months, aesthetic attributes of the site, an inventory of vacant land nearby, and ages of the buildings on the land.

There was a negative response of only 20 percent, who said they would not use such a map. They offered a variety of reasons:

- "There may be hidden deficiencies associated with the vacant land. For example, there may be people unalterably opposed to future development in the neighborhood."
- Another person said "Scattered pieces in strange places, zoned oddly, should be rezoned," so as to reflect how development in the area has actually occurred. That is, to his mind, a hidden deficiency of some parcels: out-of-date zoning designations preclude their being developed in the way market forces would seem to indicate.
- "Not in Missoula. Because the master plan misleads people, [giving them] incomplete and inaccurate information." The point here is an important one: the committed lands map must be a reliable indication of how the city and county would like to see land developed, or it will serve no purpose.
- "Limited value to a banker. Developers generally already have land

tied up." The point being made here is that development occurs at the discretion of landowners, who seek little outside guidance.

4. We have identified the following services as the ones with delivery costs that would be determined in part by where development is located:

> Primary education
> Secondary education
> Public safety (police and fire protection)
> Public works (sewers and water systems)
> Roads and highways
> Emergency health care
> Public transportation
> Miscellaneous (weed control; parks and recreation)

Can you think of other public services for which costs might depend upon distance to point of delivery?

Other important factors affected by distance—insurance rates, privately supplied utilities (gas, electricity, phone service, water), and cable television—were mentioned.

5. We want to develop a public service cost accounting sheet, so that alternative sites can be compared for public service cost efficiency.

We think such a sheet would be useful to private developers in choosing among alternative sites for a particular project. And we also think it would be useful because a reasonable cost accounting can help justify a project to the public sector.

> **a. Do you think such an accounting sheet would be useful in choosing among alternative sites for a particular project?**

There was a positive response of 26 respondents who thought the accounting sheet would be useful in choosing a site. "It can create solid information," they said, which could be used "as a basis for comparison," or for "proof" in "choosing an area most likely to succeed."

Several felt it would be useful to municipalities and public decision makers, who were looking "for alternatives to save the city money." A development justified in terms of its efficient use of civic services would "appeal to a sense of public spirit," suggested one respondent.

And finally, one person said that once a site had been chosen, the accounting sheet could then be "ammunition to get financing." And a banker said that he "would like developers to demonstrate [with a tool such as proposed here] they have undertaken a thorough process for choosing a site before the deal is set up."

There was a negative response of seven respondents who thought the accounting sheet would not be useful, remarking that a "private party won't choose according to public costs" and that "it's most useful to the governing body."

"The cost [of preparing the sheet] negates its value to a developer."

"It might not be equitable to landowners," and "It may reinforce the notion that newcomers are a burden."

One person asked a question about the logic of the notion of committed lands: "When does it allow the extension of services?"

> **b. *Do you think such an accounting sheet would be useful in building popular support for development projects?***

The majority of those interviewed thought an accounting sheet would be useful in building support for development projects, most often agreeing with one decisionmaker who said, "It could make the public aware, and prove the benefit of a project by exposing taxpayers' costs." A few qualified their agreement by saying the sheet would primarily benefit government officials forced to explain why they had approved controversial projects.

Many thought that the accounting sheet, had it existed at the time, would have helped them get approval for past developments, particularly the controversial proposals.

The negative responses arose primarily because the respondents could not realistically imagine popular support for development. As one person said, "You can never get the public behind development [because they] cannot identify future residents." And others added variations on this insight, saying, for example, "Neighborhood value overrides everything," or "[In decisions about development,] cost is not a factor, other emotional factors are more important."

And finally we were offered a thoughtful warning about using any single tool to evaluate proposals: "Support should be sought for reasons other than strictly cost; develop the support by showing minimum negative impacts and maximum positive impacts."

6. *We would like to ask your advice about when the public service cost accounting sheet described above might be useful, either to evaluate alternative sites or to use to build support for a project.*

> **a. *For what size development project do you think it conceivable that such an analysis would prove beneficial?*** *(Size could be taken to mean acreage, square footage, number of dwelling units to be constructed, or any other measure the respondent found appropriate.)* **Or, are there**

particular types of projects that would benefit from this cost accounting analysis?

"All sizes," and "all types" were the most common responses to these questions. And although some respondents gave more particular replies —dollar amounts for construction projects, or type of building—it appears that if the public service cost accounting sheet were reliably devised, it should be used everywhere and for every type of project. The crucial matter, then, will be to create a cost accounting sheet that meets the important objectives that this survey catalogued.

    b. *And finally, do you think there are any areas in this county where* all *types of development would benefit from this cost accounting? If so, where are they?*

The Rattlesnake and South Hills areas were mentioned by several people, as well as the downtown core area and lands along the city's waterfront. A few people mentioned Lolo, the lands around community hospital, Reserve Street, and the university area. More generally, some people said "everything 'outlying'," while others said "everything within four miles of the city's boundaries."

This pattern of response repeats what was found above: if the method is reliable, it should be used everywhere. A banker summarized this view: "Many economic decisions are made for noneconomic reasons because the data isn't always there. But whether it's used or not, [this cost accounting sheet] should be available."

7. *What objections do you foresee people might have to using this type of analysis?*

Many of the respondents thought that the biggest objection might come from owners of land in outlying areas, who would fear that this type of analysis might make their land worthless, or add additional development costs to their land, and thereby "destroy their dreams." Others worried that any such method would give government "too much" control.

A few respondents thought the analysis might discriminate against worthwhile projects, or that its effect would be to slow down growth; others worried it would be too costly and difficult to update. Some persons feared any additional paperwork or delays in the review process, while others felt the analysis might not be sufficiently detailed to be useful.

One person cautioned that the analysis is only interested in dollar amounts and ignores the "human element," while another said "people build on the cheapest property anyway."

8. *Can you imagine ways in which these objections can be overcome?* Many stressed the importance of public education, noting that the necessity of doing this sort of analysis must be made widely known. For example, one person said public facilities must be explained as expensive investments which entitle taxpayers to a good rate of return.

On a related note, one person said the manner in which the committed lands analysis was presented was crucial to its success, while several warned that the data on which the analysis relies must be kept current and accurate.

The maps and the analytic methods must be available to everyone. They should be put in realtors' and governmental offices, as well as in the chamber of commerce and Missoula's economic development corporation.

9. *In your opinion, what steps could local governments take to* encourage *development within the areas we're calling committed lands?* The answers here were wide-ranging, generally falling into three areas: tax incentives/disincentives; governmental participation in the development process; and more reliable review of developers' proposals.

   a. Tax incentives/disincentives:
> • Reduce taxes for development on committed lands. Most respondents mentioned this factor, although a few warned that tax reductions, once in place, are hard to rescind. And several people noted that tax reductions have the effect of penalizing existing businesses that did choose to build on committed lands—because established concerns would be paying a higher effective rate than those more newly built.
> • Enact tax disincentives, or impose developer exactions for projects outside committed lands.

   b. Governmental participation in the development process:
> • Some people had in mind actual governmental funds being used to let developers know the city and county were themselves committed to using the committed lands. For example, one person suggested an "initial subsidy up front to developers in committed lands;" another suggested "recruiting developers for these lands."
> • Others thought less expensive participation would be suffi-

cient inducement, mentioning "regulatory breaks," "help with sewer development," "free services," and so forth.

- And finally, governmental support might take the form of "governmental advocacy of beneficial projects;" or, more simply, it might take the form of wide dissemination of techniques to find sites in committed lands—sites understood as those most likely to win official approval.

c. More reliable review of developers' proposals

- While many specifics were offered, the point they made was actually a simple one: enact clear rules, and then "play by them," i.e., make decisions consistently. To the extent possible, the respondents agreed, developers in the committed lands should have removed for them "the risk factor in the approval process."

- In addition, some people emphasized the necessity of coordination among deliberative bodies, specifically between the city and county.

APPENDIX C

RESULTS OF THE
MONTANA POLL

The Committed Lands Project was interested in the attitudes of Montana's residents about regulation of land development, about encouraging development in already urbanized lands, and about where they live. When the Bureau of Economic Research at the University of Montana conducted an edition of its periodic Montana Poll during the fall of 1987, the project contributed several questions (listed below) in order to study and then work with those attitudes.

1. Do you agree or disagree that:

   a. Regulation of land development—such as zoning laws and reviewing subdivision plans—is an important government activity because it protects the safety, health, and beauty of a community.

   b. An individual's right to develop his property is generally more important than the public's interest in having that right regulated by the government.

   c. The location of new development will affect the cost of the public services that your taxes pay for.

2. How would you feel about your community having a policy of encouraging that any new development be located within the urbanized area *rather* than in the outlying rural area—would you agree or disagree with such a policy?

3. Suppose your community had designated areas where it wanted any future development to go. How would you feel about granting a tax break if a developer builds in the designated areas rather than somewhere else?

4. If it could be shown that the costs of public services would go *down* if apartment buildings and mobile homes were located closer to single-family houses, how would you feel about locating these types of housing closer together?

5. Land development regulations in Montana currently require two hearings—first, a hearing before the planning commission, and then a second hearing before either the city council or the county commissioners. Some people have recommended having only one hearing, in order to simplify the process. How do you feel about that?

6. If you could live anywhere you wanted in your county, would you

prefer to live in an area like the one you live in now, or in a more urban area, or in a more rural area?

7. We know that people can have different reasons for wanting to live in one area over another, and we'd like to know what is most important to *you*. If you were deciding now, and could live wherever you wanted in your county, would it be most important to you to have public services—such as schools, road maintenance, and so on—that are *convenient*; to have public services that are of *high quality*; to be in a *prestigious* location; to be in a *healthy* location; to be in a location that has *open space* or is *scenic*; or do you like or prefer where you are living now?

The following demographic characteristics of the respondents were determined as a preliminary phase of the poll:

- **County of residence,** for comparing the attitudes of those people who live in larger versus smaller counties in Montana[1];
- **Regional location within Montana,** to see if there is a difference in attitudes between residents of Montana's Western, Hi-line, and Southern regions[2];
- **Urban versus rural residence** (based on the respondent's description of where he/she currently lives);
- **Length of current residence;**
- **Political preference or leaning** (Democrat, Republican, Independent);
- **Age of respondent** (18–34, 35–44, 45–64, 65 and older);
- **Income level** (under $15,000, from $15,000 to $34,999, $35,000 and over); and
- **Education** (some or no high school, high school graduate, some college, college graduate).

This appendix summarizes the results of the poll, with the responses for each question organized into the following categories:

1. The overall percentage of agreement and disagreement among Montanans.

2. Differences in agreement that show a significant correlation with demographic characteristics of the respondents.

3. Demographic factors which were not correlated with different degrees of agreement (that is, the overall response for all Montanans does not significantly change when these demographic factors are taken into account).

POLL QUESTION 1a: Regulation of land development—such as zoning laws and reviewing subdivision plans—is an important government activity because it protects the safety, health, and beauty of a community.

I. All Montanans:

	Agree	Disagree
	81.4%	14.3%

II. Groupings that showed significant differences from the above percentages:

A. County of residence:

	Agree	Disagree
Seven largest counties:	86.4%	10.2%
Other Montana counties:	74.6%	19.7%

B. Urban versus rural residence:

	Agree	Disagree
Urban:	84.3%	11.6%
Rural:	79.3%	16.7%

C. Income:

	Agree	Disagree
Under $15,000:	74.4%	17.8%
$15,000–$34,999:	85.3%	14.0%
$35,000 and over	87.8%	11.2%

D. Education:

	Agree	Disagree
Some/no high school:	68.0%	16.0%
High school graduate:	79.7%	15.7%
Some college:	86.8%	12.3%
College graduate:	84.4%	13.3%

III. Insignificant factors for Question 1a:
- Regional location within Montana
- Length of residence
- Political preference or leaning
- Age

POLL QUESTION 1b: An individual's right to develop his/her property is generally more important than the public's interest in having that right regulated by the government.

I. All Montanans:

	Agree	Disagree
	63.5%	31.6%

II. Groupings that showed significant differences from the above percentages:

A. County of residence:

	Agree	Disagree
Seven largest counties:	58.3%	36.6%
Other Montana counties:	70.5%	24.9%

B. Urban versus rural residence:

	Agree	Disagree
Urban:	58.1%	35.9%
Rural:	68.5%	28.6%

C. Political preference:

	Agree	Disagree
Democrat:	55.0%	36.3%
Independent:	76.7%	19.8%
Republican:	65.2%	32.9%

D. Education:

	Agree	Disagree
Some/no high school:	66.0%	24.0%
High school graduate:	72.5%	22.2%
Some college:	64.9%	33.3%
College graduate:	45.6%	48.9%

III. Insignificant factors for Question 1b:
- Regional location within Montana
- Length of residence
- Age
- Income

POLL QUESTION 1c: The location of new development will affect the cost of the public services that your taxes pay for.

I. All Montanans:

Agree	Disagree
68.6%	20.8%

II. Cross-tabulations showed no groupings with significant differences from the above percentages.

POLL QUESTION 2: How would you feel about your community having a policy of encouraging that any new development be located within the urbanized area rather than in the outlying rural area? Would you agree or disagree with such a policy?

I. All Montanans:

Agree	Disagree
55.6%	33.3%

II. Groupings that showed significant differences from the above percentages:

A. Urban versus rural residence:

	Agree	**Disagree**
Urban:	53.5%	34.3%
Rural:	58.6%	32.5%

B. Age of respondent:

	Agree	**Disagree**
18–34:	58.8%	33.6%
35–44:	50.5%	42.4%
45–64:	56.8%	30.6%
65 and older:	54.5%	24.2%

C. Income:

	Agree	**Disagree**
Under $15,000:	54.3%	31.8%
$15,000–$34,999:	62.0%	30.0%
$35,000 and over	49.0%	44.9%

D. Education:

	Agree	**Disagree**
Some/no high school:	48.0%	24.0%
High school graduate:	59.5%	31.4%
Some college:	58.8%	35.1%
College graduate:	48.9%	40.0%

III. Insignificant factors for Question 2:
- county of residence
- regional location within Montana
- length of residence
- political preference or leaning

POLL QUESTION 3: Suppose your community had designated areas where it wanted any future development to go. How would you feel about granting a tax break if a developer builds in the designated areas rather than somewhere else?

I. All Montanans:

	Agree	**Disagree**
	64.3%	29.4%

II. Groupings that showed significant differences from the above percentages:

A. County of residence:

	Agree	**Disagree**
Seven largest counties:	65.5%	31.1%
Other Montana counties:	62.4%	27.2%

B. Urban versus rural residence:

	Agree	Disagree
Urban:	66.7%	27.8%
Rural:	62.6%	31.0%

C. Age of respondent:

	Agree	Disagree
18–34:	67.9%	26.0%
35–44:	69.7%	29.3%
45–64:	59.5%	33.3%
65 and older:	56.1%	30.3%

III. Insignificant factors for Question 3:
- Regional location within Montana
- Length of residence
- Political preference or leaning
- Income
- Education

POLL QUESTION 4: If it could be shown that the costs of public services would go *down* if apartment buildings and mobile homes were located closer to single-family houses, how would you feel about locating these types of housing closer together?

I. All Montanans:

Agree	Disagree
48.8%	48.0%

II. Grouping that showed significant differences from the above percentages:

A. Urban versus rural residence:

	Agree	Disagree
Urban:	47.0%	51.0%
Rural:	50.2%	45.8%

III. Insignificant factors for Question 4:
- county of residence
- regional location within Montana
- length of residence
- political preference or leaning
- age
- income
- education

POLL QUESTION 5: Land development regulations in Montana currently require two hearings: first, a hearing before the planning commission, and then a second hearing before either the city council or the county commissioners. Some people have recommended having only one hearing, in order to simplify the process. How do you feel about that?

    I. All Montanans:

	Agree	**Disagree**
	47.0%	46.8%

    II. Grouping that showed significant differences from the above percentages:

        A. Urban versus rural residence:

	Agree	**Disagree**
Urban:	44.4%	48.5%
Rural:	49.3%	45.8%

    III. Insignificant factors for Question 5:

- county of residence
- regional location within Montana
- length of residence
- political preference or leaning
- age
- income
- education

POLL QUESTION 6: If you could live anywhere you wanted in your county, would you prefer to live in an area like the one you live in now, or in a more urban area, or in a more rural area?

    I. All Montanans:

	Same	**More urban**	**More rural**
	64.5%	5.9%	28.9%

    II. Groupings that showed significant differences from the above percentages:

        A. Urban versus rural residence:

	Same	**More urban**	**More rural**
Urban:	61.6%	6.1%	32.3%
Rural:	68.0%	5.9%	25.6%

        B. Age of respondent:

	Same	**More urban**	**More rural**
18–34:	52.7%	6.9%	38.9%
35–44:	63.6%	4.0%	32.3%
45–64:	73.0%	3.6%	10.6%
65 and older:	74.2%	10.6%	15.2%

III. Insignificant factors for Question 6:
- County of residence
- Regional location within Montana
- Length of residence
- Political preference or leaning
- Income level
- Education

POLL QUESTION 7: We know that people can have different reasons for wanting to live in one area over another, and we'd like to know what is most important to *you*. If you were deciding now, and could live wherever you wanted in your county, would it be most important to you . . .

I. All Montanans:

36.3%—To be in a location that has *open space* or is *scenic*.

23.3%—To have public services, such as schools, road maintenance, and so on, that are *convenient*.

20.6%—To be in a *healthy* location.

13.7%—To have public services, such as schools, road maintenance, and so on, that are of *high quality*.

2.7%—Like/prefer where I am.

1.0%—To be in a *prestigious* location.

II. Groupings that showed significant differences from the above percentages:

A. County of residence:

	Seven largest counties	Other Montana counties
Open space/scenic:	35.3%	37.6%
Convenient services:	24.7%	21.4%
Healthy location:	22.1%	18.5%
Quality services:	14.5%	12.7%
Like where I am:	0.4%	5.8%
Prestige location:	0.4%	1.7%

B. Regional location within Montana:

	Western	Hi-line	Southern
Open space/scenic:	37.9%	40.4%	32.5%
Convenient services:	17.1%	22.2%	29.0%
Healthy location:	26.4%	17.2%	17.8%
Quality services:	10.0%	13.1%	17.2%
Like where I am:	4.3%	5.1%	—
Prestige location:	1.4%	—	1.2%

C. Urban versus rural residence:

	Urban	Rural
Open space/scenic:	30.3%	41.9%
Convenient services:	28.8%	18.7%
Healthy location:	23.7%	17.2%
Quality services:	13.1%	14.8%
Like where I am:	0.5%	4.9%
Prestige location:	1.0%	1.0%

III. Insignificant factors for Question 7:
- Length of residence
- Political preference or leaning
- Age
- Income level
- Education

The robust collection of data summarized in this report indicates that Montanans have a strong commitment to the following: an individual's right to develop his/her property, a preference for rural living, and the preservation of rural areas. Those respondents living in rural areas and in the state's smaller counties felt more strongly about these values than did residents of urban areas or larger counties.

Especially interesting to the committed lands research team were the cross-tabulations between responses to different questions. For example, almost 60 percent of the respondents who agreed that an individual's right to develop property was more important than land use regulation also agreed that growth should be guided into urban areas rather than allowed in rural locations. And of those respondents who did not think land use regulation was an important governmental activity, 50 percent agreed that new development should be located within urbanized areas (while 43 percent disagreed), and 53 percent agreed with locating mobile homes and apartments closer to single-family houses to save service costs (while 41 percent disagreed). That is, even though these respondents apparently did not agree with the idea of government regulation of land uses, they apparently thought *some* control should be exercised over how land gets developed. From these apparently anomalous responses, it appears that Montanans' individuality and preference for rural living could be offset by the cost savings and preservation of rural areas afforded by development in committed lands.

NOTES

1. The seven largest counties in Montana are Yellowstone, Cascade, Missoula, Gallatin, Lewis and Clark, Flathead, and Butte-Silverbow. Each has more than 35,000 inhabitants. Montana's other 49 counties each have fewer than 25,000 people.

2. This regional distinction was determined from Ellis Waldron's 1924–1980 index of party preference. Those counties in the Western district are Anaconda-Deer Lodge, Butte-Silverbow, Flathead, Granite, Lake, Lincoln, Mineral, Missoula, Powell, Ravalli, and Sanders. The Hi-line district includes Blaine, Cascade, Chouteau, Daniels, Dawson, Fergus, Glacier, Hill, Judith Basin, Liberty, McCone, Phillips, Pondera, Richland, Roosevelt, Sheridan, Teton, Toole, and Valley counties. The Southern district includes Beaverhead, Big Horn, Broadwater, Carbon, Carter, Custer, Fallon, Gallatin, Garfield, Golden Valley, Jefferson, Lewis and Clark, Madison, Meagher, Musselshell, Park, Petroleum, Powder River, Prairie, Rosebud, Stillwater, Sweet Grass, Treasure, Wheatland, Wibaux, and Yellowstone counties.

APPENDIX D

OUTLINE OF RULES OF PROCEDURE FOR PROCEEDINGS BEFORE A HEARING EXAMINER

I. Definitions
- Applicant
- Party
- Local government
- Governing body
- Departmental staff
- Local ordinance
- State law
- Hearing examiner
- Ex parte communication
- Clerk

II. Ex parte Communications
- Initiated by member of the public
- Initiated by hearing examiner
- Remedy

III. Hearing Examiner as Presiding Official
- Qualifications
- Appointment
- Removal
- Conflict of interest
- Disqualification and replacement
- Independence

IV. Powers and Responsibilities of Hearing Examiner
- Prescribe rules of procedure
- Hold conferences
- Administer oaths
- Issue subpoenas
- Allow oral and written testimony
- Prohibit or limit cross examination
- Rule on motions and other procedural items
- Regulate the course of the hearings and the conduct of parties
- Rule on, receive, exclude or limit evidence
- Abbreviate hearing's normal sequence of events
- Fix time limits
- Limit number of witnesses and length of testimony

- Take official notice of facts
- Question any party presenting testimony
- Make final decisions and/or recommendations to governing body
- Report periodically to governing body

V. Nature of Proceedings
- Frequency and schedule
- Computation of time
- Prehearing conference
- Informal format
- Expeditious proceedings
- Trip to inspect land
- Burden of proof
- Rules of evidence
- Limits on testimony
- Public comment period
- Record of hearing

VI. Rights of Applicant and Parties
- Due notice
- Due process
- Testimony
- Limited cross examination
- Objection
- Motion
- Legal counsel

VII. Elements of Hearing
- Hearing examiner's introductory statement
- Report of departmental staff
- Testimony of applicant
- Testimony in support
- Testimony in opposition
- Cross-examination (if allowed)
- Rebuttal
- Questions by the hearing examiner

VIII. Hearing Examiner's Docket
- Application
- Staff report
- Public comments
- Evidence received

- List of exhibits
- Matters officially noticed
- Findings of fact
- Conclusions tied to law
- Decision or recommendation

IX. Content of Staff Report
- Names and addresses of landowner and applicant
- Summary of the requested action
- Common and legal descriptions of property
- Technical data summary of the property
- Current and proposed access to property
- In-depth analysis of project and its impact from the perspective of statutory criteria
- History of requested action and development in the surrounding properties
- Summary of any other requested land use permits in the area
- Summary of the reports and recommendations of other agencies
- Appropriate maps
- Summary of public reaction to proposal
- Staff's conclusions

X. Other Procedures
- Withdrawal of application
- Continuation of hearing
- Reopening hearing and reconsideration
- Appeal

Index